The
Christian
jesus

Also by Kenneth Cragg and
published by Sussex Academic Press

*With God in Human Trust – Christian Faith and Contemporary
Humanism*

The Weight in the Word – Prophethood: Biblical and Quranic

The Education of Christian Faith

Faiths in Their Pronouns: Websites of Identity

Readings in the Qur'an

The Christian Jesus

FAITH IN THE FINDING
Kenneth Cragg

THE *Alpha* PRESS

BRIGHTON • PORTLAND

2 4 6 8 10 9 7 5 3 1

First published 2003
in Great Britain by
THE ALPHA PRESS
PO Box 2950
Brighton BN2 5SP

and in the United States of America by
THE ALPHA PRESS
5824 N.E. Hassalo St.
Portland, Oregon 97213-3644

British Library Cataloguing in Publication Data
A CIP catalogue record for this book is available from the British Library.

Library of Congress Cataloging-in-Publication Data
Cragg, Kenneth.
The Christian Jesus : faith in the finding / Kenneth Cragg.
p. cm.
Includes index.
ISBN 1–898595–42–9 (alk. paper)
1. Jesus Christ—Person and offices. I. Title.

BT203 .C74 2003
232—dc21
2002153041

Typeset and designed by G&G Editorial, Brighton
Printed by MPG Book Ltd, Bodmin, Cornwall
This book is printed on acid-free paper.

Contents

Prefatory Note

Books are always at the mercy of their readers who may well misread. That is the risk they run when pen ventures into print. It often happens so when the themes are religious and times liable to prejudice. Hence the need for authors to be alert for the misunderstandings they may incur.

There are two areas here about which to be preventive. One is that 'The Christian Jesus' is a naïve or pretentious title, the other that it intends to say 'not a Jewish Jesus'. There is no ground to either.

The first charge would be that we only have '*a* Christian Jesus' to lay our private claim. There are numerous versions of 'The man from Nazareth'. None can be definitive. Indeed, there has always been 'division because of him'.

Likewise there have been many 'revolutions' and many 'constitutions', but it is still intelligent to talk of 'the French Revolution' or 'the American Constitution'. For there was something – in both cases – intimately bonding between the two words so that using 'a' or 'an' would make quite other sense. The conviction here is that 'the Christian Jesus' is a similar usage. A faith possessed him with its adjective in terms to which his name belonged. If, in truth, he might be 'many' he could be only this way. So faith believed. Its case needs careful, gentle making.

Anti-Semitism is so rank an evil that against it there must be a perpetual vigilance. 'The Christian Jesus' would be party to such vigilance. There is here no voiding or evading of 'the Jewish Jesus'. That Jesus was supremely Jewish has never sanely been in doubt. He has the 'Christian' descriptive inside the binding reality of the 'Jewish'. It was from the very heart of 'Jewishness' and its 'Messiah' that he and his immediate Jewish disciples gave to human history a confidence concerning 'God in Christ'. It was a confidence instinctively and rightly called 'Christian'.

Gratitude is meant to the sources, mainly poets, from whose writings quotations have been drawn.

That He whom the sun serves
should faintly peep

Through clouds of infant flesh:

That He, the old eternal Word,
should be a child and weep:

That He who made the fire
should feel the cold:

That heaven's high Majesty His court should keep
in a clay cottage . . .

That glorie's self should serve our griefs and feares
and free eternity submit to years.

Richard Crashaw, Poetical Works, Edinburgh 1857, p. 38

Saluting the Memory of
The Central College of the Anglican Communion at Canterbury
1948–1967

Opus Fidei
Labor Caritatis
Somnium Tradebatur

Introduction:
How and Why 'Christian'?

Jesus has had many descriptives out of long history. Some would say that 'the Jewish Jesus' is the only valid one. Never in intelligent question, that verdict is fully embraced in the 'Christian' one. The question always was: 'What manner of Jew?' For fourteen centuries there has been 'the Muslim Jesus', with anthology drawn from the Qur'an and Tradition presenting their picture with an emphasis on 'one who had nowhere to lay his head'. Doubtless one can visualise 'the Hindu Jesus' gathered into the instincts of India and its crowded pantheon.

If we wanted a phrase like 'the English Shakespeare' it would have to be 'the Galilean Jesus' or 'the Palestinian Jesus', as – in local terms – the Nazarene. Then, however, the very accuracy would leave too much unsaid. But is 'the Christian Jesus' saying too much? If so, it would be as faulted as saying too little. Could it ever be like proposing to talk about 'the Dickensian Dickens' – which no one would do because it would be mere repetition? What is 'Christian' anyway is far from being a unanimous matter, so perhaps '*a* Christian Jesus' is the most we could duly say. Could even that be authentic?

We have come upon an issue implicit in all religions, if not – in some measure – involved in all reported history, namely that facts of 'reading about' the actual (if we ever have it) become, in turn, 'facts of the situation'. Facts of belief *are* facts with which we have to reckon. It is, therefore, vital to ask why and how 'what was' yielded the eventuating account, or verdict, about it. Even if 'disreputable', the 'reported to be so' is another event. That historic Christian faith canonically housed in New Testament documentation arrived, via Jesus-authorship, is a fact of history. That it validly did so is a fact of belief: whether it validly did so is an issue of discourse and decision.

Hence the sub-title here: 'Finding it so', which is carefully different from 'wanting it so' or 'making it so'. We are committed to exploring how it happened that, from the ministry and significance of Jesus there developed this historic faith *about* him as due faith *in* him and authentically *from* him. This faith-community certainly ensued. It placed in history 'the Christian Jesus'. Its grounds lay deep and far in the nature of God and the fabric of human experience as evident in selfhood and society.

This meaning of 'the Christ in the making of Christians' was, historically, a profoundly Jewish thing. For it had to do with this Jesus being 'the Christ' – 'Christ' being the Messianic response of God to the wrongness of the world. It was a response identified – as the very making of the Church – in all that Jesus, in perceived Messianic capacity, had meant and suffered and achieved. Only so did the name 'Christian', whether as his or theirs, become apt and true. The acceptance of Jesus, in those divinely Messianic terms, drew the name from the very text of his story.

It took some little time for the 'Christian' word to arrive and overtake earlier ones about 'the way', 'the fellowship', or 'disciples' and 'believers'. These it readily absorbed and maintained in inclusive relevance. In the ultimate coining of 'Christian' they had captured the mutuality between a Lord to love and a 'body' to comprise. They were a people of Jesus' making because he was the maker of their faith as his people. Their destiny lay in embracing the destiny his Messiahship had in them. Such was the reciprocal thing at the heart of all else, the intelligible, the intelligent, warrant of the word 'Christian' as fully designating both Jesus and a church bearing his name and sign. In Johannine language: 'I in them and they in me . . . that the world may know.'

'The Christian Jesus', thus found so in Christian faith, is loyal and honest only in taking up, in due course, the deep reservations anticipated in the 'Prefatory Note' and broached in Chapter Six. They are best measured in the positive setting where hostility kindles and misgivings arise. But 'Messiah'[1] being the kindred term, all hinges on how radically, how extensively, how realistically, its reach is read both as identify in history and as capacity in God. Our best hope and our truest wisdom is to relate all we can inside the defining word.

'The Christian Jesus', then, found so in Christian faith. Story into faith, faith out of story, suggest a certain progress in exploring how they inter-belong, namely through salutation as with music, in perception of the sacramental, via the readiness of motherhood, by the drama of ministry and the Passion, from the criterion of Scriptures and the issues of controversy, to the finality of love's possession.

Chapter One turns to poetry in the telling. There is a long tradition that it was on a cloud of songs that the divine Word accepted Incarnation. For in all its quality of paradox, of form and meaning, that Word was 'poetic statement', where – beyond mere prose which indicates – there is expression that conveys with a kindling art. Rime and rhythm, assonance and metre, are fit partner for the truth they carry, where thought is tuned to soul. So it was in 'Word made flesh', bringing poetry to its heeding as more prompt and true than creed. Theology, likewise, is first debtor to doxology and belief begins in adoration.

Disquisitions, still more controversies, can bide their time while a music of celebration salutes the Christ nativity, savoured through a wealth of poets in their mastery of verbal wit and reverent worship. The Incarnation was well calculated, in 'the conception of the Holy Spirit', to search out and sift in human hearts the tributes of their dexterity, their transferred metaphors, their Latinisms or their devout fancies and, more deeply still, the wonder of a transcendence stooping to their verbal offering.

If there was lively hymnody, reportedly, in heaven, around the birth of Jesus, there were hours of silence round his crucifixion. Yet, in prospect and in retrospect, the silence has been broken by the poetic voice of faith. Few events in history have had the sound of verse and music more richly in dirge, lament, contemplation and a wondering awe than the Passion of Jesus crucified. Jeremiah's 'How does the city sit solitary' may have drawn an emulation but the 'look and see' concerning Jesus and the Cross has no parallel in all religion.

It is, then, for thoroughly interior reasons, an impulse at the heart by which 'The Christian Jesus' takes faith first into poetic strain, not – as some would see – in self-persuasion, but in love-persuasion that moves art with it into gratitude and wonder.

Sincerity in one dimension has to mean integrity in another. It is imperative to 'love the Lord with all the mind'. Where faith becomes lyrical it needs also to be honest about the ways and nature of God. What must the Christ story have been to have had the sequel thus possessed? That sequel, clearly, *was* the faith itself. What was it understanding in its will to psalmody?

Answer takes us to Time's sacrament. The word from its Latin origin, with the sense of 'minding as holy', had its root far back in the Hebraic tradition concerning divine action identifiable, because experienced, at points in history where the Hebrew people knew it for what it was, and were summoned by it to awe and worship – and, with these, a strong assurance about themselves.

There were points in time where divine action was intimately associated with the human scene. In the strict grammatical sense of those familiar phrases 'the God of Abraham', 'the God of Jacob', He was – as it were – 'possessed' by these patriarchs in that His infinite reality bore actively on their circumstance of nomadism or of patriarchy and could be situationally known by them in personal terms. 'The God of Israel . . . visited and redeemed His people'. Time, or times, 'presented' Him in that they made Him present. What happened for Jacob at Bethel and at Peniel

[3]

made those locatable times to become for him 'God's house' and 'God's face'. Events on the human side were a sort of lectionary where His text could be read.

This Hebraic faith about God in action for them was 'sacramental' about time, in being – as the very term implies – a 'counting sacred', a transaction between the activity of God and the human awareness that perceived it so. The human side (if we may so speak) contributed the responding recognition. The divine part was in evoking it by acting relevantly to the immediacies of a human 'there-and-then', in Abraham's case his wanderings with a sense of promise to a guided destiny, in Jacob's the tensions of his ambition and his twinned bond with Esau.

Sacrament always has this dual character – a discernible or discerned 'time' of God and the experience it humanly confers. The Exodus from Egypt became the supreme 'time' of that association with Yahweh – as from thence He could be called – for those who passed out of bondage under Moses. They had been assured that Yahweh would 'be there' and 'there' in those terms. The tradition of the Passover ritual could ensure that the memory of it would 'through all generations' decide their theology.

How this sacremental sense of time passed into Christian reckoning with the meaning of Jesus of Nazareth is the task of study in Chapter Two as underwriting all poetic telling and setting in its frame all the chapters that must follow. It had its continuity into Christianity through the long vicissitudes of Messianic expectation in anxious sequence from the Exodus and ever disputed destiny into the Incarnation of 'the Word made flesh', where 'the Word' is a profoundly 'speaking' deed 'minded sacredly' in and as the New Testament.

For the destiny read and assured in the Exodus went at length tragically awry in the Exile. It had duly ushered its people, as promised, into the land and the land had duly enjoyed its ultimate David in kingdom and Temple. But Solomonic power did not endure except as a legend of proverbial wisdom. The kingdom divided, had many cycles of decay and hope until both north and south finally succumbed to brutal powers from the east and the long 'weeping by the rivers of Babylon' ensued.

Human tragedy inside pledge of divine election could only engender some vindication of the one in the pained perplexity of the other. The 'I will be there' as pledged at the Exodus argued some 'where Yahweh will be' in respect of national suffering and of hope frustrated. Through many phases and readings that awaitedness about God's action in answer to Hebrew experience of tragedy was 'Messiah', out of the 'root of Jesse', that is, in essential 'sonship to David'. The words about Exodus, relating heaven to human bondage: 'I have seen . . . I know . . . I am come down to deliver . . .' (Exodus 3:7) would need to have their logic again somehow in the light of Sennacherib and Tiglath-Pileser and what they did to Israel and Judah, more devastating than any Pharaoh. He had wanted to bar them from land and promise: they had depopulated land and derided promise.

So Messianic hope must resolve the riddle in righting the wrong and be, for that very destiny, a riddle in itself concerning the how and where and when and who of its fulfilment. It would be the supreme sacrament of how Yahweh 'minded' the sacredness of His people and where they could 'mind' His answer. Either way, it would be about a coming, an intervening, a descent from heaven, a tenure upon earth, a tenancy of God inside a human span of time. Had not the God in Exodus said: 'I am come down to deliver'?

When, as we explore in Chapter Four, a faith emerged convinced that this hope had been made good, against all seeming 'not so', in Jesus and his Passion, it instinctively told itself in that 'I am come down' language and borrowed that perception of a defining tenancy in time – defining because redeeming, just as 'redeeming' was the language about exodus and exile.

It is sometimes held that Christian faith about the divinity of Christ derived from pagan, Roman precedent where Empire 'divinised' the Emperors the better to ensure popular veneration of the State and thereby the subjugation of the people. The 'nativity-festivals' were the artful propagation of this imperial sleight of hand. It was both useful and festive that Caesar could be made divine.

'Twas odd that any parallel could be alleged. The Biblical was all the other way – not a fictive exaltation of the human proud but a purposeful descent of the divinely generous. That sovereignty, inviolate already from eternity, was not contriving to secure itself but bending to fulfil itself. Divine transcendence has this self-expending quality in pursuance of the self-outgoing capacity evident for all Semitic minds, Biblical and Quranic, in the creation and our common, commissioned creaturehood within it.

'Time's sacrament', then, read in 'the Christian Jesus' by a faith finding it there, necessarily became a theme of a 'descending and ascending Lord'. If Incarnation had transpired then it was out of what had always been so and would always so remain – in a 'Christ' for ever 'pre-existing' in the nature and being of God and for ever post-existing there, seeing that the earthly sojourn was the expression of that being. That 'pre-' and 'post-' applied because time is of that sort when it is involved. No 'incarnation' has happened if the physicality is eternal. What enters through birth 'descends' from its eternal priority: what supervenes after death 'ascends' thither again. It is time that requires what seems like an 'episode' about

God but, in that constraint of divine grace, it has the nature of eternity. It begins and ends only that it may abide for ever – 'God in Christ reconciling the world'.

Such in the theme of Chapter Two – 'time's sacrament' as Christian faith finds in its Christian Jesus. It is not rightly seen as any aberration of what should properly be otherwise. The impulse to its logic is deep in Hebraic tradition about a Lord who acts, whose transcendence stoops to human association with history and its contents and, for Christianity, history's contents most realistically read and pondered. Of Christ's Incarnation it is bold to say:

> . . . now I have answer from the face
> That is the place
> Where all I touch is moved to an embrace.

Arriving there is to come first to a nativity.
As an early carol has it:

> In His byrth holy was knytt
> God and man in his degre,
> Moder and mayd together were sett
> Forth in man's harte ever to be.

So Chapter Three belongs to Mary and Magnificat. Her Song is the surest place in which to appreciate her person and her role. For, as a poet said elsewhere and of another lyric, 'It has the assurance of a rose'. 'Mary, full of grace' is not well 'hailed' as a gratuitous source of virtue to bestow but only and truly as an exemplar of how the divine wills to employ the human. She must always be seen as yielded into the vocation she perceives as waiting for her readiness but gently seeking it. She is handmaid to the birth that is the time pre-requisite of incarnation. 'It was his love's prerogative to come by need of her'. For, birth apart, no more follows.

Her annunciation, then – as G. M. Hopkins (1844–89) knew with sure instinct in his poem – is the invitation to all discipleship.

> Minds me . . . of her who . . . Gave God's Infinity,
> Dwindled to Infancy, welcome in womb and breast,
> Birth, milk and all the rest . . .

John Ruskin, in his *Fors Clavigera*, thought that what he called 'the worship of the Madonna' had been never other than 'productive of true holiness of life and purity of character'. That could indeed be so, but without 'other than'. For there have sadly been forms of 'the Madonna' that came near to idolatry and darkly shadowed the meaning of the Son she bore and, thereby, the mystery of her bearing him. Truly 'calling her blessed' stays within the measure of her – and our – 'magnifying' of the Lord. Chapter Three means to do so in musing on other duties around our faith in 'virginal nativity', never meant as sheer marvel for marvel's sake, so that we have to suspend all questions or offer them on an altar of the credulous. Rather they are held inside the fuller context of the Incarnation as the ever wondrous speaking deed of God as Word.

This New Testament faith takes us where Mary ever points, to the actuality of this enterprise of divine presence at its sacramental point in history. It is best captured in the emergent phrase with its strong possessive: 'Our Lord Jesus Christ', where creeds themselves had birth. They told – inside their whole theology – of a person fulfilling an office and describing a standing. The words belong in any order because they inter-define what each separately tells. They come naturally in the New Testament Letters. The Gospels come into being to narrate their story. By these means we have them (see Chapter Five) 'according to the Scriptures'. Such these will become because of him.

That phrase, however, and that 'accordance' reach back into the early anticipations of 'Messiah' as the time-and-person point of divine action in a history awaiting it. It is vital that faith duly possesses and rightly tells how the awaited was the realised, the promised the fulfilled. That reading of events around Jesus held promise and fact in one. It will be the heart of the 'argument' of 'the Christian Jesus' that he was such as to bring about what it came to hold and that what it came to hold he brought about. There was this necessary mutuality between him in the drama and the faith finding him so. If we use a risky current word from philosophy it was a 'construct' of the faith's which his event-in-story had 'constructed' for them and for which, in the telling, they found the language of Biblical tradition from advent to ascension. Or, in the idiom of the Exodus, the Lord had 'truly been there as there He had been' and 'been' in this Jesus, coming, dwelling, leaving, in the abiding quality of 'grace and truth'.

What tells itself as 'according to the Scriptures' is the witness of faith about its own origin, an origin traced out of promise and taken to climax by events. We have to reckon with how the disciples came by the conviction as to Jesus crucified that made them into apostles of his resurrection. All might be caught in the old carol refrain:

A wonder thing it is to see
How lord and servant one may be.
Was ther never nonne but he.

Ministry out of Nazareth has to be seen as one with the compassion and tears of Gethsemane and both with the entering into 'glory'. Incarnation did not mean, simply, that 'a child is born', but also that 'a son is given', the son who 'comes preaching', and 'teaches' supremely both of God and ourselves, in the inclusive lesson of the Cross and all that faith believes ensued in his 'departing', with the 'exaltation' as a frontier on transcendence, even as nativity had been in inauguration.

All had been – for ever is – divinely 'episodic', as God's 'here-is-now' and 'now-is-where' about the human scripting of His nature to make us 'literate' with faith. But 'literate' means having all within its own dimensions of birth and death, of advent to the one and ascension beyond the other, of the Mother Mary and the empty tomb, the meaning of the womb, the vacancy of the sepulchre, the risen-ness of Jesus as the Christ and 'the Lamb in the midst of the throne' – all frontiers either way and the signifying territory between.

There is an immediate and obvious sequel to all these meanings of the study made in Chapters Four and Five – the 'Disputanda' in Chapter Six. 'Things that call for refutation' might translate the Latin term. To be sure, there are many such on many grounds. Nor should faith want to evade them. It is its health, not to say its instinct, to await them, being no conspiracy to silence about the misgivings it might arouse. Its content is too precious to forego adequate measure, just as it is too distinctively shaped to be taken for granted. Moreover, throughout history there have been many distortions of its meanings and tensions in its expression.

Chapter Six, therefore, has to meet scepticisms or disquiet on a wide front. There are those that find the 'Jesu, lover of my soul' language inordinately self-centred and who read in Christian theism an impossible quest for 'the Holy Spirit the Comforter' in a supposed sense of that 'comfort' word it does not have and will not bear. To think to find, or even to seek, 'the Saviour' – they argue – is to want what is not honestly to be had and would be destructive of moral integrity if it were. Agnosticism, by this count, is the only true courage, while faith in Christ is the refuge of the craven-hearted. To be truly moral we must look for no reward but take a disinterested stand on our selfhood against the delusions of the religious mind.

Such is a philosophical indictment of perceived salvation. It often allies with current aspects of 'literary criticism' to suggest the 'human construct' account of religious faith as being 'all in the mind'. Reading anyway, these days, is hostage to readership, language being no more than a game with signs – a view superlatively so when the language ventures into a metaphysics or a theology it can never convey. A 'construct' is always prey to 'deconstruction' and Christianity, being an improbable one, is the more probably so fated. Even atheism no longer needs to be aggressive, nor assertive since all things tend towards vacuity.

Christian theology, of course, has allies in facing down this kind of mental 'melt-down'. It is, however, seen at heavy disadvantage among secularists by reason of its perceived 'myths' around Mary's womb and that 'empty tomb', with somehow half-embodied 'appearances' of a risen Jesus who ate with disciples but passed through walls unseen.

'Myth', of course, has long been a mischievous word, if – in such phrases as 'the myth of God incarnate' – there was nothing save fantasy or dream or invincible illusion. If, however, we appreciate its technical sense, it is a term that will profoundly signify. As Chapter Two explains, 'sacrament' is preferred here to denote that 'frontier situation' which must be present and understood *ex hypothesi* of any sacrament in time and history believed expectable from God. Birth and dying are the parameters of any divine enterprise of incarnation. For time and humanity and mortality condition it. Then 'virginal nativity' at the outset and, through death, exaltation from the mortal scene, might be witness to an authentic sojourn, whose content and achievement were commensurate with the given divine purpose. Then those 'frontiers' would be contained in the faith that had honest ground for conviction about the whole they enclosed within themselves, namely the Incarnation and the Passion for whose entire sake they had defining moment and decisive meaning.

'Disputanda' has a duty to develop further the cares the sceptics bring. At all events, we can get beyond the stance that talks of baulking at miracle, if we realise there was never present what would require it. Christian faith is not like some Jewish *eruv*, a fenced area in which we hold suspended the laws by which we would otherwise be bound, of scientific norm and evidence, laws with far better writ than the fastidious rulings of a Torah. There is no such *eruv* of suspension of disbelief in the right quality of faith the Incarnation and the Passion have us bring to them. Divine initiative is all.

These areas apart, there are duties for 'Disputanda' from witnesses to 'the Jewish Jesus' who through the last century have entered into New Testament debate with deep erudition and sometimes militant controversy, determined to rescue 'Jesus the Jew' from Christian annexation or monopoly. These vital matters reach into inter-Christian and other scholarly discussion about the Gospels, the Epistles and the emergence, inside that first quarter century of the Christian faith, of the *Carmen Christi* of Philippians 2:5–11, about 'descent even to death on a cross' and 'high exaltedness' into 'the Name above all names'.

These perennial duties of scholarship to faith and of faith towards scholarship are made the heavier for our time by the steady hardening of the cultural heart against the practice of reverent worship and by the trivialisation of the mind and neglect of 'the things of the Spirit'. The strictures earlier noted on the alleged cowardice of belief seem the more odd when it takes such courage to believe. So many factors conspire to undermine convictions that are less than robust. An inept frivolity attaches to much journalistic comment on the themes of religion so that the cares of mind and spirit they demand are wanting and depreciation is the more entrenched.

In this climate, faith's presentation suffers some loss of necessary nerve when it falls back, for lack of one, on sheer assertion, or takes refuge in emotional sanctions that convey only to themselves, or seeks refuge in liturgical fidelity and becomes thereby the more a private option. Then secular summary of its actual nature is too often seemingly confirmed by the excesses of fanaticism which evoke a nausea for all practitioners of the transcendent. An irreligious world would be a happier, safer planet, provided we could be morally adequate enough. Moral adequacy, however, is never exempt from the religious principle of 'minding things sacredly'.

It may be relief to turn in Chapter Seven, finally, from these stresses and strains of 'Disputanda' to 'Love in Possession'. Not 'relief', however, if only as 'escape', but rather as the better apprehending, and being apprehended by, 'the Christian Jesus'. For something reciprocal is ever in mind. 'Jesu, joy of man's desiring', 'Here would I stay and sing' – these will only be half of it. For their other half is 'Confirm my heart's desire to work and speak and think for thee'. 'Finding it so' makes the *Adeste fideles* of the Latin carol for each and all a singular summons to that 'pearl of great price' whose purchasing takes 'all that a man has'. 'Here will I stay and serve'.

CHAPTER ONE

Poets in the Telling

"Poetry is the first and last resource of Christian faith." Doctrine only intervenes. Otherwise, how could it be that song and praise have always been among the arts of worship or that, as long tradition had it, the divine Word came to Incarnation amid a chorus of seraphic celebration reportedly audible over the fields of Bethlehem?

This situation is, of course, highly suspect to the carers for logic and the guardians of intellect who demand the rigours of the syllogism and despise the license of the lyrical and mystical. Their cautions need respect. For there are evident disciplines controlling the liberty with which music moves and tells. Poetry, too, can be ready for the questions but let its will to ardour and surrender first be heard. Faith can better admit of argument when its vision has been seen, its inner wonder sensed. For these remain prior in their meaning when the case concludes.

Having celebration prior enables a soul imagery to express the language of the Incarnation, the *Verbum Dei caro factum est* of Christian theology, first measured here as poetry's theme before we pass to 'Time's Sacrament', 'Mother's Enabling' and the rest, to come at length to 'Love's Exchange . . .'. Splendid examples avail in the idiom of the so-called 'metaphysical poets' of the late 16th and early 17th centuries. Among them was Richard Crashaw. The lines from his *Sacred Verses* set out on p. vii are variations on the theme of transcendent lowliness, the self-expending of 'the unmeasured God' clad in 'a few poor rags', weeping infant tears, when 'free eternity submits to years'. The sundry metaphors shape into the oddly royalist paradox of 'One keeping court in clay cottage' open to all the winds that blow.

Crashaw writes inside the tradition of John Donne, George Herbert, Henry Vaughan, Francis Quarles and many lesser lights. It was a pattern of writing which contrived a lively intercourse between the manner and the substance of its word-play so that the theme was contrived to fulfil itself in the very texture of its expression. The technique – if aptly so termed – is known to literary criticism as a 'conceit' which is, of course, very close to 'conception', and so well set to tell in *Sacred Verses* the theological one which was the Incarnation. 'Conceits' transacted themselves in sharply fitting meaning to expression by deliberate choice of arresting incongruities, by perceptions of association the more striking for being abnormal, bizarre, even exotic or grotesque. In consequence the hearer or the reader was compelled to a new quality of attention precisely in being shaken out of the familiar by dint of the far-fetched. The art of conceit worked by conjuring an incredulity to gain a credence.

This 'court in clay cottage' might thus do better justice to Incarnation than: 'Now the birth of Jesus was on this wise . . .' A different 'this wise' is devised the better to tell the prosaic one. Christian theology, at its soundest, has always been involved in such 'conceit' about 'virginal conception' and the *Ave atque vale* explicit in a Lord who is said to 'come' who also says: 'It is expedient that I go . . .' Chapters Two and Four must turn to that necessity of 'time and the eternal', which Richard Crashaw read as 'royal court in human clay for cottage'.

Like all his fellow poets he rejoiced in paradox – as does the faith in 'Word made flesh'. Indeed, tending to, or ending with, paradox is implicit, paradox being the last haven of analogy, as where 'the Eternal Word' is, as infant, 'unable to speak a word'. Such are Crashaw's verses. 'Be ye my fictions: But her story' he could say of his lines 'to his (supposed) mistress'. In *Steps to the Temple* he could bizarrely link his 'blushes' to Christ's 'own heart-blood'. These literary excesses, however, do not detract from the worth and impact of his surer lines, full in the metaphysical tradition of wit and epigram, as when he defined 'hope' as 'the entity of things that are not yet', where 'Our nothing hath a definition'. Or when, in *A Hymn of the Nativity sung by the Shepherds*, he has 'full chorus' tell

> . . . all wonders in one sight!
> Eternity shut in a span,
> Summer in winter, day in night,
> Heaven in earth and God in man;
> Great little one! whose all-embracing birth
> Lifts earth to heav'n, stoops heav'n to earth.

where the very paradox of Christian theology is minted into the ready currency of poetic faith when neither can suffice without the other.

Richard Crashaw (1612–49) was well-placed to know about 'courts', both academic and royal. His father, one time preacher at The Temple in the Strand and a noted Puritan divine, had seen him, his only child, to Charterhouse whence he arrived at Pembroke College, Cambridge, whence again to be a Fellow of Peterhouse. There he moved from his father's legacies to be 'higher' Anglican in the Laudian pattern then prominent at Peterhouse. During the tensions of the thirties of the century, of Laud's ascendancy and Charles I's 'absolutism' leading to the Civil War, he took the journey John Donne had taken in the opposite direction and became a Roman Catholic, though he had shared for a while in the community of Little Gidding.

One factor in the story may have been his becoming chaplain in Paris to the court of Charles' Queen Henrietta Maria. Italian influences came in his later years when his poems found publication (1646). But the course of his travels between England, France, Holland and Rome, with sojourns in Oxford and Leiden, is unclear. Whatever his capacity, private or public, Crashaw was familiar enough with those royal progresses of court with which the genius of Elizabeth I graced her sovereignty and intimated it across the realm to the great arousing of her subjects' awareness and her claim upon their minding. They were the 'where' and 'when', the 'here and now', of majesty brought home to country house and civic folk. They were her way of telling them how her 'weal and woe' were ever one with theirs, how she and they were authentic to each other in the due bonds of authority and grace.

When an Elizabethan royal progress took to the road the court was indeed a 'visitation'. Bells swung in the steeples, pageants filled the streets and the populace was feted with masques and due and worthy pomp. It was as if the realm itself travelled to make local what was never absent – that rule of power which brought its other dimension in the circuit judges of the sovereign's peace. Through their writ the 'Crown' took over the jurisdiction of any subject's 'cause' or 'quarrel'.

Crashaw's father could well have witnessed the splendid progress south from Berwick on Tweed that James I of England made with leisurely speed to his Westminster Coronation. His reign saw many local forays in the shires, as if renewing that 'presenting to the people' which opened its solemn ritual, being thus an 'acclamation' in dispersal. Richard Crashaw's Cambridge, and then court connections, readily brought these images to mind as he pondered on the other majesty of Jesus as 'incarnate Word'. The theologians of that 17th century were deeply preoccupied with how *regio* went with *religio*. Like many of his fellow poets, with a life-span of hardly four decades, he knew how 'winged time's chariot' and by its close had sensed the disappointments of his world – a situation which may explain the extravagances of his imagination, not least in his Latin verses.

Whatever the material fortunes of his twilight years in Italian exile, or the despondency they may have brought, his spirituality allowed itself a wide verbal indulgence only because it was deeply rooted in its Christian ground. Excesses in its usages may be forgiven in the reach of his perception into faith. As for others of his nurture and instinct, the effort after language was the ardour of the faith that needed it, so that 'conception' as language and as conviction was happening together. He reached the language as he grasped the faith as mutually party to its truth. Or, as his Shepherds' Hymn sang:

> We saw Thee and we blest the sight,
> We saw thee by thine own sweet light.

Had not the psalmist (36:9) said: 'In thy light we see light'? The second line has summed up a theology of the Incarnation. Does Crashaw disserve it when he lets his excess of celebration further enbellish the line with these six:

> Gloomy night embraced the place
> Where the noble Infant lay,
> The Babe looked up and showed his face –
> In spite of darkness it was day!
> It was thy day, *sweet*, and did rise,
> Not from the East but from thine eyes?

Conceit, indeed! as your literary critic will opine and yet the poet's fantasy contains faith's cognisance of how 'face' and 'dawn' might teach each other and a cerebral *confessio* has found its music.

Crashaw's practice of the art of believing poetically is at its surest in the lines on 'the unmeasured God'. Infancy is duly there again but now likened to the sun, which elsewhere Crashaw has reproached for absence in the 'night' of Bethlehem. Now he has it shining through the clouds – clouds that clothe and somewhat hide the light which they, even so, diffuse, the sun that, never absent is presently obscured 'in infant flesh'. So bold is the imagery that the willing mind is compelled to pause at its incongruity and so sift its plea to be allowed, when a livelier surrender ensues.

All concerns 'unmeasured God' so that the poet is obliged to range far for proper 'measures'. 'Sink' is an intransitive verb: 'low' echoes Mary's 'low estate'. Was the divine quest of the human, somehow, willed indeed as 'stoop' will later tell, also moved by a law of condescension that could not fail to happen? Either way, the 'unmeasured' is being told.

'Swaddling clothes' do indeed imprison but Crashaw's 'few poor rags' do scant justice to Mary's careful homespun competence, except that they are 'few and poor' for what is royally due. Tears are never far away from cradles but they come from 'eternal Word', from a babe whom Galilean 'clouts' ill preserve against the winter cold in Judea – and bring the poet again to the sun, the only 'fire' to dispel the 'cold' of the earth-dwelling where the Eternal comes.

And so to 'court in clay cottage' as the residence of this 'high majesty'. Crashaw was familiar enough with the Book of Job and 'them that dwell in houses of clay whose foundation is in the dust' (4:19). 'Our bodies are bodies of clay' (13:12), earth their raw material, decomposing from felipathic rocks and readily mingling with water to take whatever shape a potter will or to bear the imprint (38:14) of whatever seal awaits it. If the poet had Shakespeare's Lear in mind on 'the blasted heath', Lear discovered 'unaccommodated man' in the bitter desolation of an old age wilfully beset by folly, clinging wretchedly to a royal status he had only formally relinquished. Here the blasts that 'controlled' the poem's royal babe (or, as modern speech would say 'buffeted') belonged with an inauguration.

With 'glory's self' Crashaw reported the sum of all that theology of the Incarnation defines as for ever sealed in 'serving human griefs and fears' and then, in every sense the crowning line: 'And free eternity submit to years'. 'The Word made flesh' has been told in 'words made meet' for the telling but only so because the meaning sensed had brought the words to birth in confession of poetic soul. All is as if the poet, like some not yet aged Simeon, has taken up into his arms the child he understands and tells us he has 'seen his salvation'. Such, in the devotion that theology finds through words, is indeed what the literary critic calls 'conceit', but as a soul's mind born of perception and telling the truth it learned. Such poetry is, therefore, in itself a kind of incarnation where the human is taken into the divine yet only by a capacity the divine has evoked. It is 'the Word' that draws these words by which to tell itself anew and in them yields itself to dwell in the emotion they convey.

Thus, a sort of nativity transpires when poetry comes to human birth, giving form to what the soul received. How apt, then, that incarnation into human shape and reach should be the language of divine employ in love to humankind. This seems to be the burden of William Alabaster's *Incarnatio est maximum Donum Dei* in which he blends the (first) word into the double sense of humans in poetic cognisance of the natural world – and God's ultimate gift of Himself in human terms.

> . . . God's eternal bounty ever shined
> The beams of being, moving, life, sense, mind,
> And to all things himself communicated . . .

in all the evidences of earth and time apprehensible to human wit and wisdom

> But see the violent, diffusive pleasure
> Of goodness that left not, till God had spent
> Himself by giving us himself his treasure

[15]

In making man a God omnipotent.
How might this goodness draw our souls above
Which drew God down with such attractive love.

'Omnipotent man' has the characteristic extravagance of the metaphysical poet, yet pardonably so, in celebrating what so magnanimously empowers our theological awareness of divine grace. 'Attractive' has, clearly, both a descriptive and a transitive sense.

Such was the confidence about being authentic in and by this faith that argued the kind of logic Richard Crashaw reached in his 'Charitas Nimia' among *Steps to the Temple*. He queries the case for any divine interest in the human realm.

Lord, what is man? Why should he cost thee
So dear? What had his ruin lost thee? . . .
What have his woes to do with thee? . . .
Why should a piece of peevish clay plead shares
In the Eternity of thy old cares? . . .
If I were lost in misery
What was it to thy heav'n and thee?

He reasons that, all redeeming expenditure apart, heaven would stay eternally serene, 'thrones and dominions still adore' and 'ever wakeful sons of fire keep warm his praise'. 'Should not the King still keep his throne?' At length his prayer moves out of this perceptive rhetoric to cry: 'O make me see how dearly thou hast paid for me!' to end with the lively paradox:

That *lost* again my life may prove,
As then in *death*, so now in *love*.

The theme of divine infancy inside the faith in the Incarnation hallows the mystery of all human childhood. This was a note central to the poetry of Henry Vaughan (1622–95), a self-confessed disciple of George Herbert, who ponders his own infancy as somehow still near the inner side of eternity which – as Wordsworth also thought – our coming towards adult awareness sadly forfeits. The mystery of a childhood which God shared (in the nature of the Incarnation as faith knew it) confirmed those intimations of meanings all birth possessed and all 'experience' surrendered, when of mortality made conscious. Did 'the eternal Word,' through an infancy humanly growing into the articulate manhood of ministry and the Cross, bring again for us what our tenancies of time had lost in coming from where that loss belonged? If our childhood had been 'close to God', God's own childhood brought Him close to us, though not without the deeper closeness of the Cross.

'Shadows of eternity', Vaughan cried, 'O how I long to travel back' from the 'weaker glories' my waning sight can 'spy', 'to see again eternity!' He is ready to set this sense of things at the heart of the call of Christ to his first disciples, after their own question: 'Rabbi . . . where dwellest thou?' He thinks their enquiry must have been:

> . . . did some cloud
> Fixed to a tent, descend and shroud
> My distrest Lord? or did a star . . .
> . . . haste gladly down
> To lodge light and increase her own?

The imagery is alive with natal things, John's loved 'tent' (1:14) and Matthew's 'guiding star'. The poem continues:

> My dear, dear God! I do not know
> What lodged thee then nor where, nor how:
> But I am sure thou dost now come
> Oft to a narrow, homely room,
> Where thou too hast but the least part,
> My God, I mean my sinful heart.

He seems ready to ignore all the familiars of 'where' and 'how' – at Bethlehem, by Mary – to have his own self the place and means. Some two centuries later, Christina Rossetti would come by the same question: 'What shall I give him, poor as I am?' The emotions of love-theology are contagious.

Henry Vaughan is bold to carry that theme of disciples in discovery to the story of Nicodemus, the Rabbi who 'came to Jesus by night'. Doing so again he overrides narrative constraints. He has the 'night' bestow a sufficient light 'as made him know his God by sight', illumined instantly by the Christ to whom he turned 'as glow-worms shine and face the moon'.

> Most blest believer he!
> Who in that land of darkness and blind eyes
> Thy long expected healing wings could see,
> When thou didst rise:
> And, what can never more be done,
> Did at midnight speak with the sun.

His conceit matches that of Richard Crashaw and outruns the real story in the zeal of its imagination. Yet it communicates, not in spite of its excesses but because of them.

Thomas Traherne (1634–74) stands much loved among 17th century contemporaries for his sensuous delight in external nature and the human body as affording every self an 'annunciation', in the vocation to be responsive to a would-be presence. His prose works (*Centuries of Meditations*) have a peculiar fascination by reason of their 20th century 'discovery' after nigh fifteen score of years lying away unknown. His poem 'The Return', like many more of his, muses with Henry Vaughan around a sense of lost innocence.

> To Infancy, O Lord, again I come,
> That I my Manhood may improve:
> My early Tutor is the Womb:
> I still my cradle love.
> 'Tis strange that I should wisest be,
> When least I could an Error see.

Yet the body in full mature awareness is the place of an 'annunciation' to the self, so that Jesus' Incarnation could be known as a truth of our humanity as well as of divine grace. Traherne sang.

> . . . their useful eye,
> Their precious hands, their tongues and lips divine,
> Their polisht flesh where whitest lilies join
> With blushing roses and with sapphire veins,
> The bones, the joints . . . various limbs that living engines be
> Of glorious worth.

Dylan Thomas' 'green fuse driving' is of the same wonder and 'time held' him 'green and dying', being 'golden in the mercy of his means'. Or Traherne, elsewhere, addressing himself:

> Thy treasures
> Abide thee still, and in their places stand
> Inviting yet, and waiting thy Command.

Supremely in that physicality is the gift of coition and the partnership of pregnancy entrusted to our flesh. Of this an anonymous 14th century poet, known as 'The Pearl', writes as fit to be minded sacredly, granted to our flesh by the 'King who rules in his court . . . so honourably served', who

> Made them natural means . . . communicated secretly . . .
> A manner of mating of marvellous sweetness.
> In my brain (he said) was born the embrace of lovers.

This poet is one, two centuries later, with George Herbert's 'all things may of Thee partake' – a truth of us forever ensured in 'One who took our nature upon him'. If Edmund Spenser (1552–99) asks, in *The Faerie*

Queen, 'And is there care in heaven, and is there love . . . That may compassion on their evils move?' the answer is the affirming of Jesus in that very task.

It is intriguing how Crashaw's 'king and court' imagery about the Nativity seems instinctive. Richard Southwell (1561–95) had savoured it a little earlier in his carol:

> This stable is a Prince's court, This crib his chair of state,
> The beast are parcel of his pomp, The wooden dish his plate.
> The person in that poor attire, His royal livery wear,
> The prince himself is come from heaven,
> This pomp is prized there.

He has played on paradox with less subtlety but conveys how it belongs with equal charm.

John Donne, Dean of St. Paul's (1572–1631) and held as 'master of the metaphysicals', was at one point Rector of Sevenoaks in Kent, where a resident and 20th century poet, C. H. Sissons (1914–), summons him in satirical lines to encounter its men today in their High Street, on their station platform. The faith at his St. Nicholas (the Parish Church) Sissons tells him 'is not exclusive of the fools it chooses'. Even 'the highly sexed are the natural prey of the incarnate Christ'. The irony is worthy of the once lascivious 'Jack Donne', who had written much about 'folly' both before and after his conversion and who saw himself as 'captive to Christ'.

'Christ's prey' is fair metaphor for the 'conceits' of poets and the sentiment of carols, capturing his Incarnation in the web of their imagination. A right theology might think that 'prey' thus happens in reverse. He is captive to them in the care of their devotion. Such is evidently the case in Christina Rossetti's 'bleak midwinter carol' where love is inventive and theology incautious. Yet, in the carol tradition, how could they be otherwise? The frost and ice and snow are quite gratuitous. They owe themselves to midwinter celebration and probably – as did T. S. Eliot – to the sermon of Bishop Lancelot Andrewes in Whitehall in the presence of James I: 'A cold coming they had of it at this time of the year, just the worst time of the year to take a journey . . . the weather sharp . . . the very dead of winter'. As for 'snow had fallen, snow on snow,' so evocative in scene and sound, did it inspire the loaded imagery in James Joyce's 'The Dead', where 'the snow was falling all over Ireland . . . snow falling faintly through the universe'?

Inter-association is so far a part in the service of literature to faith. 'A stable place suffic'd' – rhyming words for 'Christ' are all too few – was Christina Rossetti's contrast with a 'heaven' that 'could not hold him' (contain? or retain?) and an 'earth' that would dissolve at another coming? She told the paradox superbly but her 'doctrine' faltered in being both right and wrong. 'The Lord God Almighty, Jesus Christ' could not be so simply in apposition, if the Incarnation was understood.

For 'Jesus the Christ' was indeed 'God Almighty' but in the meaning of 'incarnate Word' from un-vacated heaven. The meaning of identity with God was only so as being the image of the Father and thus requiring the 'differential' within the one identity by which alone historic Incarnation could transpire or be understood. God, like an author, *is* what He authors, as with 'musician' and 'music': (these being, e.g. the same 'Beethoven') if the shape of the unity is understood. The point belongs more fully in Chapter Two. The poem is altogether authentic in the will to celebrate, telling with an art to engage all willing souls. Divine nativity begins to be understood.

Andrewes had this sense of things by a bold metaphor in another Christmas sermon when he said:

> The Sun of righteousness (Malachi 4:2) entering into his eclipse begins to be darkened in His first point, the point of His Nativity.

In the sun's transcendence there is no 'eclipse' except one that hides only in order to reveal in issue from a strange concealment. But, as the preacher adds: 'This holds good with the ensuing course of His life and death'. Christmas only celebrates inauguration. The 'stable place' did not suffice. Nazareth, a synagogue, hillsides, country lanes, the temple court, the Mount of Olives, a garden called Gethsemane – all these would share what could suffice, and on to a 'place called Calvary' and a 'road to Emmaus'. For, as Simeon says in T. S. Eliot's 'A Song for Simeon', 'the Infant (was) the still unspeaking and unspoken Word'. The 'poets in the telling' would stay with him all the way.

In his wistful style A. E. Housman (1859–1936) caught the opening places of 'sufficing' for the Lord in self-expending.

> It was in fair Bethlehem, There came a merry crowd,
> They stopped before the stable door,
> And knocked thereon aloud.
> 'Oh, open, open,' cried they then,
> 'As wide as wide can be:
> Heart of Jesus, suffer us to come to Thee.'

Robert Graves (1895–1985) pointedly imagines Jesus in the wilderness temptations 'answering brotherly' 'lost desert folk, that listened wonderingly', among them the gaunt 'old scapegoat', who 'tears like a lover wept'.

The calling of the disciples beside the sea has kindled many a poetic

muse, of nets whirled like the skirt of a dancer, to sink slowly downward
in a catch and be drawn ashore to greet a figure standing there promising
a catch of men through a will to follow. Richard Crashaw plays with his
customary wit on such a call to Peter.

> Thou hast the art on't, Peter, and canst tell
> To cast thy nets on all occasions well:
> When Christ calls, and thy nets would have thee stay,
> To cast them well's to cast them quite away.

Despite – for the most part – the disciples' raw simplicity, the 'court'
metaphor keeps recurring as with Thomas Washbourne (1606–87).

> He did men invite, by gentle means.
> Twelve of the simpler sort
> Served to make up his train and kept his court.
> Not chance, but choice, did first apostles make:
> Christ did not them at all adventures take.

The versifiers pass to the teacher in the teaching, with Edmund Spenser
'considering the lilies', 'no man for them taketh pains or care, yet no man
to them can his careful pains compare'. The lily

> Neither spins nor cards, nor cares, nor frets,
> But to her mother nature all her cares she lets.

As for Solomon and 'all his glory', Abraham Cowley (1616–87) has 'his
royal southern guest, of Sheba' looking up 'to roofs of gold',

> and nought around could behold but silk and rich embroidery . . .
> (but) wealthy Hiram's princely dye . . . and
> She herself and her gay host were dressed
> With all the shining glories of the East . . .

till, walking into the palace garden, she found

> Every rose and lily there did stand
> Better attired by nature's hand.

So the poets drew their education from incarnate Word and conjured
others into school. Giles Fletcher (1588–1623) knew this Galilean
'educator'.

> He is a path if any be misled,
> He is a robe if any naked be,
> If any chance to hunger, he is bread,
> If any be a bondman, he is free . . .

To dead men life is he, to sick men health . . .
A pleasure without loss, a treasure without stealth.

George Herbert with ready wit muses on the warning from Jesus about 'idle words' (Matthew 12:36) and advises:

Pick out of mirth, like stones out of thy ground,
Profaneness, filthiness, abusiveness:
These are the scum with which coarse wits abound . . .
All things are big with jest; nothing that's plain
But may be witty, if thou hast the vein.

Commenting on 'why are you so fearful?' (Matthew 8:26), Crashaw reinforces the point of the story.

There is no storm but this
Of your own cowardice, that braves you out.
You are the storm that mocks
Yourselves, you are the rocks of your own doubt.
Besides this fear of danger, there's no danger here.

Is it not part of the meaning of the Incarnation of the Word that it so readily recruits, and finds occasion for, the language skills of heeding men?

'Lord, I am legion', 'the hem of his garment . . . if I may but touch', 'under my roof not worthy', 'Let us go to another village' – all these have spelled their meaning into other words, 'made flesh' again in mind and music. We can say, with William Blake (1757–1827), of this:

The soul awakes, and wondering sees
In her mild hand the golden keys.

Or, with Robert Browning (1812–89) on 'the cup of cold water' (Matthew 10:42) given in Christ's name

. . . because it was my heart I proferred,
With true love trembling at the brim,
He suffers me to follow him.

God 'registers the cup' and 'disdains not His own thirst to slake'. Or, with Henry Vaughan on 'seed growing secretly (Mark 4:27):

Dear, secret greenness! nursed below
Tempests and winds and winter-nights,
Vex not, that but one sees thee grow,
That One made all these lesser lights.
Then bless thy secret growth, nor catch

at noise, but thrive unseen and dumb:
Keep clean, bear fruit, earn life, and watch
The white-winged reapers come!

Or, how sane old Francis Quarles on the spared, if barren, fig tree.

Judge not too fast . . . Hast thou not patience to expect the hour
Thy judgement oft may tread beside the text:
A Saul today may prove a Paul the next.

The same poet compares Mary and Martha and their roles in Bethany.

Mary sat silent, hears but speaks no word:
Martha takes all, and Mary takes no pains:
Mary's to hear; to feast him Martha's care is.
Now which is greater, Martha's love or Mary's? . . .
Sure, both loved well: but Mary was the debtor,
And, therefore, should, in reason, love the better.

What lively sight Quarles had of that chief publican, Zaccheus! He
pictured him climbing 'with a busy haste' the concealing tree that would
hide his ill repute and serve well his little stature, but in his descending 'he
ne'er made trial if the boughs were sound', 'by such a spirit driven'.

Down came Zaccheus, ravished from the tree:
Bird that was shot, ne'er dropt so quick as he.

In all these situations 'poets in the telling' give us lyrical appreciation of
the meaning of the Incarnation. By very nature, 'the Word made flesh'
was complete in the history: that completeness – also by its nature – could
find perpetuating expression of its fulness via the wit, the wealth, the
worth of its cherishing in those apt for mediation of their vision. Choice
here, in a single language tradition, shares with many others whom it
represents, 'the greeting of the spirit' in love to the Christ of their conviction and the magnet of their souls.

Just as 'poets in the telling' dwelled so long in the Nativity, so they
moved instinctively towards the Passion. As for pilgrims afoot, so for
poets apace, 'the road to Jerusalem is in the heart', just as with the
'psalmists of ascent' (Psalms 121–129), not, now, as those who thought
to 'prosper' but as those who would be 'acquainted with grief'. There was
something inexorable about the moving into tragic climax of Jesus'
ministry. The disquiets of authority concerning him, the counsels of prestige, were like a gathering storm that, unless evaded by compromise or
flight, would break over him and his. 'Murmurings' rumbled round his
parables and while there was popular acclaim which he would not exploit,

authority would find a way of circumventing it, maybe by co-operation from within his circle and by dint of an astute diplomacy. That inner 'handing over' could be concerted, it would seem, out of an impatience – in at least one of his followers – about the tardy, languid fashion of his promise of Messiahship, so that if it were 'treason', it stemmed from Jesus' own failure to make good his Kingdom in its awaited terms. Then, either way, whether by antipathy towards, or disillusions within, his band of frail and faltering men, the die was cast, the tragic would ensue.

That progress of Jesus' ministry, from cumulative benedictions of word and benefactions of deed, into its culmination of suffering, was vividly legible, on both counts, in the Palm Sunday entry, where 'the cleansing' of the Temple captured its whole active logic and precipitated its dramatic climax. How well the lines of the learned Jeremy Taylor (1613–67) sensed its double force. Yet he only does so by turning it inward to the personal self where all disciples kneel, all mortals hallow or degrade.

> Lord, come away: why dost thou stay?
> Thy road is ready, and thy paths made straight,
> With longing expectation wait
> The consecration of thy beauteous feet.
> Ride on triumphantly: behold we lay
> Our lusts and proud wills in thy way.
> Hosanna! welcome to our hearts. Lord, here
> Thou hast a temple too, and full as dear
> As that of Sion, and as full of sin;
> Nothing but thieves and robbers dwell therein.
> Enter and chase them forth and cleanse the floor;
> Crucify them, that they may never more
> Profane that holy place
> Where thou hast chose to set thy face.
> And then if our stiff tongues shall be
> Mute in the praises of thy Deity,
> The stones out of the temple-wall
> Shall cry aloud, and call
> Hosanna! and thy glorious footsteps greet.

The drama of that day found voice in three other contrasting tributes in verse. Charles Wesley (1707–88) was sure that in the throngs of Galileans there (did they not possessively acclaim him as their 'prophet of Galilee'?) came plaudits from his sundry beneficiaries, travelling with him to the capital. Wesley summons them to cheer as erstwhile in their sorry plight, now walking, hearing, seeing by their liberation.

> Hear him, ye deaf, His praise ye dumb
> Your loosened tongues employ:

Ye blind behold your Saviour come,
And leap, ye lame, for joy.

It was a glad conflating of the years.

Memorably, G. K. Chesterton (1874–1936) offered his poetic talent to the donkey, prime participant and crucial clue to the event.

When fishes flew and forests walked
And figs grew upon thorn,
Some moment when the moon was blood
Then surely I was born.

With monstrous head and sickening cry,
And ears like errant wings,
The devil's walking parody
Of all four-footed things.

The tattered outlaw of the earth,
Of ancient crooked will:
Starve, scourge, deride me: I am dumb,
I keep my secret still.

Fools! For I also had my hour;
One far fierce hour and sweet:
There was a shout about my ears
And palms before my feet.

The lines say nothing of the rider: the silence holds a telling magic.

The 'hour' meant verses of another order for the ecclesiastic, Henry Milman, authoring one of the finest hymns in the English language (1791–1868) and capturing the theme in the fivefold mandate from the thronging crowd: 'Ride on, ride on, in majesty', as if assenting to the urgency of the right Christ has in proof. 'Pursue thy road with palms and scattered garments strewn.' It is a drama of inauguration, set to 'lead captivity captive', and unfolding in the awed vigilance of heaven, as 'the last and fiercest strife.' The hymn is properly bold, like Rossetti's carol, to call this Jesus by the ultimate name his Passion verified as duly his.

In lowly pomp ride on to die:
Bow thy meek head to mortal pain,
Then take, O God, thy power and reign.

'Pomp' suggests a Victorian world and the irony is less skilful than a Donne might venture or a Herbert quaintly reach but Milman's lines carry into Holy Week an awed devotion of the heart. Richard Crashaw found three with which to close it on Holy Saturday, addressing the Jesus of the sepulchre.

How life and death in thee agree.
Thou hadst a virgin womb – and tomb.
A Joseph did betroth them both.

Poets from every Christian century have lived between those betrothing Josephs. In coming to poetry of the Passion it may be well to start from Edwin Muir's vision (1887–1959) of 'the Cross undone' and Jesus ever-more 'uncrucified', 'discrucified', 'his agony unmade, his cross dismantled'. This rumoured sequel will not be till 'time is ripe', 'ripe' only when he is 'wanted'. Then 'Glad to be so – the tormented wood will cure its hurt and grow into a tree'. Judas, too, will 'take his journey backward from darkness into light and be a child beside his mother's knee'. Betrayal will be 'quite undone'. This – as the poem's title ran – will be 'The Transfiguration'.

It is not a Biblical vision yet not one which Christian doctrine – from which Edwin Muir always kept a reverent distance – can well ignore. 'Transfiguration' in the Gospel had the coming crisis in Jerusalem for theme, when Jesus talked with Moses and Elijah, as with law and prophet-hood. Was Muir thinking that 'remembering by the wounds' in 'bread and wine' would be obsolete 'when he comes', and his own 'presence' would supersede them? Yet faith had it that the 'presence' would be 'this same Jesus', whose wounds were the insignia of his glory. To have 'suffered these things' had always been understood as partner to the Lordship. Could the insignia change or be withdrawn? 'Has he marks to lead me to him?' had rightly been the question of the desert Father, Stephen of Mar Saba and all his kindred. 'The throne of God and of the Lamb' (Revelation 22:1 and 3) – one throne, 'the Self-Giver's in the Self-giving' – had always been the truth of things. What the Incarnation had manifested it had neither originated nor terminated: the love it told had been eternally the nature of God and would eternally so remain.

So the poets of the Passion cherish and possess, in the aptness of their art, the divine 'poem' of Christ's Cross. Edwin Muir himself proved a penetrating searcher of the Incarnation and grieved over human betrayals in the Church of

The Image, and the Incarnate One . . .
Whose chose this form and fashion for our sake.

It was a 'form and fashion' that embraced the hurt and tragedy of human wrong and in the 'mind' of that embrace took and absorbed it in forgive-ness, so breaking the hold both of enmity and shame, and liberating from the wrong. That 'wrong', so taken in the Cross, was not some accumu-lated 'mass' from eras of gathered sins. That, in the nature of time, could never be. It was, and could definitively be, wrong in its essence, its tragically perennial character, institutional, social, personal, 'sin not sins', as history contained and could not circumvent it. Only forgiving love could take what its redemption must require and take inclusively. Love of that order and capacity was love in its divine expense – expense of which the Passion of the Christ was point and proof.

Knowing it so would not, could not, mean our return to innocence, nor think such love 'discrucified'. The experience of redemption in the human tells its counterpart in the Christ-likeness of God and of God in that enduring Christ-likeness. The faith that learns it so responds to the love that made it so, and the Passion finds a poetry kindled in its fire.

There was much poetry already in psalm and prophet whence much of the narrative found a ready language of phrase and theme. Jeremiah's Lamentations could teach it how to grieve. 'Look and see . . .' would pass into 'When I survey . . .'; 'Ho every one who thirsts . . .' into 'all ye who seek for sure relief . . .'; 'Grieve not for me . . .' has John Donne sure that 'this beauteous form assures a piteous mind'.

The familiar turns of phrase: 'betrayed with a kiss', 'it was about the third hour', 'darkness over all the land', 'let us see whether . . .', 'lots for his garment', 'it was without seam woven . . .', stay pointedly in the memory and live again in tributary verse. The Gospels are more reticent than the poets about the experience of sweat and wounds and the agony of nerve and sinew in the body's flesh. Nothing dream-like can speak into some 'Dream of the Rood', or John Donne write well, for mere rhyme's sake, of 'hands which span the poles . . . peirc'd with these holes'. Isaac Watt's 'His dying crimson like a robe hangs o'er his body on the tree' is too far a flight of fancy from 'the wondrous cross'. Yet somehow its very excess helped him to his authentic conclusion in the 'demand of love so amazing, so divine'. It is the way of poets to take extravagance into the proper modesty of wonder, to exuberate the better to understand and speak. Or, as Donne's Holy Sonnet 9 says:

> Mark in my heart, O soul, where thou dost dwell,
> The picture of Christ crucified and tell . . .

Such telling of Good Friday, however it dwells with the crucifixion and the burial of Christ, returns ever wisely to 'the night in which he was betrayed'. Then – in the upper room – there was the next day's own poetry enacted in 'bread and wine', 'the table spread beneath his name and sign', linking alike creation and redemption. Alice Meynell (1847–1922) has both dimensions finely in her 'In Portugal' – reflecting around the ever-present, oft unsuspected 'Lord of the sacrament' where nature and the Cross invite to single celebration.

And will they cast the altars down,
Scatter the chalice, crush the bread?
In field, in village and in town
He hides an unregarded head.

Waits in the corn-lands far and near,
Bright in His sun, dark in His frost,
Sweet in the vine, ripe in the ear –
Lonely, unconsecrated host.

In ambush by the merry board
The Victim lurks unsacrificed,
The mill conceals the harvest's Lord,
The wine-press holds the unbidden Christ.

Unregarded, unbidden, unconsecrated can be said alike of the natural order and of the incarnate, and the crucified, Lord. For both wait on, wait for, the discerning recognition of the ready mind.

Was it not a will to such readiness which, via his Welsh Chapel nurture, kindled the poetry of Dylan Thomas (1914–53)?

This bread I break was once the oat,
This wine upon a foreign tree . . .

This flesh you break, this blood you let
Make desolation in the vein,
Were oat and grape,
Born of the sensual root and sap,
My wine you drink, my bread you snap.

He moves into direct address because he has come to Holy Communion inside a holy communion he has never left. For, as he said 'My busy heart . . . sheds the syllabic blood and drains her words'. The crossed analogy with tears and veins is characteristic of a poetry which – he was insistent – was meant to be 'religious'. It was exactly this awareness of the sensuous human form as 'an index of delight' and a realm of tragic risk that for ever made faith poetical, because it for ever underlay the divine strategy in the Incarnation that embraced the Passion.

'Bidden, regarded, consecrated' – to undo Alice Meynell's irony about the unminding world – faith finds Passiontide, Christ's burial and Resurrection to be the divine Word speaking its own mind in the strange music of their mystery. 'Lo, love is risen!' but, instinctively for such as A. E. Housman, 'doubting grief returns', and requires, like Thomas, to be re-assured by marking those sharp dissuasive wounds.

Except by all the wounds that brake
His heart and marred his brow

Most grievously for sorrow's sake,
How shall I know him now?

It would be part of love aptly to satisfy the yearning that had most anxiously, indeed unerringly, identified where love's claim to an answering love was most critically at risk, namely in the utter anomaly of its wounds. 'Except I see in his hands . . .' was, for the Johannine Christ, the most fitting demand of any faith truly alive to what most deterred it – namely that Calvary it had undergone. Faith could never be grounded in what most disqualified it, unless disqualification was satisfyingly disproven and disproven for evermore.

It is as such decisive mastering of doubt that we understand Christ's Resurrection. Burial, with its customary finality, was always a fact for Christian faith. 'And that he was buried' needed to be credal. Jesus' 'risenness' can only avail the future in that it assuredly clarifies the otherwise 'harrowing' past on Golgotha, that place of skulls and shame. Whatever the medieval 'harrowing of Hell', the sure 'unharrowing' through which the disciples passed after devastation post-Gethsemane, would be the larger meaning. 'He is not here' about that 'new sepulchre' had freed him into everywhere, but only 'through that grave and gate of death'.

Hymns and poems need to be suspect about too easy 'Hallelujahs'. They are the more real from deeper retrospect to the Passion.

Learn we by the wound-prints Easter understood
Why the faith of ages called that Friday good.

Where Christ's hard encounter with this world of sin
Master-minds our pardon, calls us next of kin.

This divine redeeming bides in bread and wine
Sacrament of meaning, minding His for mine.

There with love's perception find we daily bread
To His task recruited, at His table fed.

Poets here are introductory: we have to pass to more incisive and intellectual accounting of 'the Christian Jesus', to the Christology that has always been the template of Christian theology as the middle paragraph of creeds, the Fatherhood of God known in the Sonship of Jesus and both through the abiding of the Holy Spirit.

It is significant that a Thomas of the 19th century, the poet Robert Browning (1812–89), a lively merchant of lyrical querying and questioning, was – for that very reason – a most forthright voice about the Christhood of Jesus. He set squarely on belief its proper onus.

Faith in the thing grown faith in the report – Whence need to bravely

disbelieve report
Through increased faith in thing report belie?

Scepticism and faith, both, did well to interrogate themselves and either for the good sake of the other. There is ready example in Browning's 'Saul', where the young David is playing his harp to sooth the tormented king who has so much misused and envied him. David asks:

> Do I find love so full in my nature, God's ultimate gift,
> That I doubt his (God's) own love can compare with it?
> Here the parts shift?
> Here the creature surpass the Creator
> – the end what began?

He must conclude that God has the greater competence and that his own impulse compels theology to say so. Later in 'The Ring and the Book', characteristically rhetorical, Browning asks, about the 'tale' of Jesus.

> What lacks, then, of perfection fit for God
> But just the instance which this tale supplies
> O love without a limit? So is strength,
> So is intelligence. Let love be so,
> Unlimited in its self-sacrifice,
> Then is the tale true and God shows complete.

Elsewhere again in the strange tale of the 'Arab physician', Karshish, this 'grand suspicion' is held vindicated.

> So the all-Great were the all-Loving too –
> So, through the thunder comes the human voice
> Saying: 'O heart I made, a heart beats here!
> Thou hast no power, nor mayest conceive of mine,
> But love I gave thee with Myself to love,
> And thou must love Me who have died for thee.'

Love given wherewith to love 'God in Christ' was both the conviction and the motive of poets of Nativity and Passion and these from the out-going economy of 'God most high'.

> Christ's Cross and Adam's tree stood in one place . . .
> By these his thorns, give me his other crown.

CHAPTER TWO

Time's Sacrament

The *Ave atque Vale*, 'hail and farewell', that the poet Catullus inscribed on his brother's grave must seem an odd salutation to have for Eternal God, Lord of all time. 'Wilt Thou be as a wayfaring man who turns aside to tarry for a night?' the prophet Jeremiah had asked (14:8) but only because he dreaded that it might be so. Yet what we must call, if crudely, 'a physicality with dates' is at the heart of Christian faith about 'the Christian Jesus'. 'The Word made flesh' was thereby subject to the time-span of biography so that greeting for an arriving and a departing had appropriate place in any confession of an *incarnatus est*. Christianity consists in the story of a coming and a going. One who says: 'I come to do Thy will' is later saying: 'It is expedient for you that I go.'

Thus what has inauguration in motherhood has farewelling through a sepulchre that opens into an ascension. Indeed, so crucial are the entry and the exit that the Creeds mysteriously omit to register anything between.

> Conceived . . . born . . . suffered . . . crucified, dead and buried, descended into hell . . . rose again . . . ascended . . .
>
> Begotten before all worlds . . . not made . . . came down from heaven and was incarnate . . . made man . . . was crucified also . . . He suffered and was buried . . . rose again and ascended . . .

Here life and ministry, word and work, mind and meaning, are comprised and embraced inside an advent and an exaltation. As beginning and as ending, these are the requisite, the thesis, of all else.

It is not that they merely enclose, like brackets, a parenthesis inserted as incidental to a major theme. On the contrary, they are understood as the focal significance of all out of which they come and into which they go. They are like the curtain of an earthly theatre, rising and then at length falling on an authored presentation requisitioning these necessary dimensions in location of its will to be articulate on a stage and through the hours of human kind. The content of their years tells an authorship no longer hid in anonymity but offering in culmination an inclusive drama, One whose 'goings forth are from everlasting' (Micah 5:2). This incarnate Word faith understands as being one with the 'word of the Lord by which the heavens and the earth were made'.

That faith has always had a query with itself as to how the Eternal could 'happen' in this way, how the ever transcendent could be episodic, the divine be in an 'interlude', or – as Crashaw had it – 'free eternity submit to years'. Immediacies, however, are the very stuff of time which has its 'presentations', as Wordsworth said, in 'spots', in seasons, occasions, lengths and breadths, the interim 'whens' by which our days are known. These combine with explicit places which are everywhere what we humans know of space and story.

The divine in any sense intending our society, still more our urgency of need, could not exempt that aim from a curtain rising on to history, a coming in some terms where we are. For a perennial absent-ness would spell the end of any theism we might intelligibly confess or realistically understand. What could be wrong with wayfaring if we are ever to be shown the way? If, for our reasoning, there must be paradox in any eternal/temporal unison in our history the paradox must lie in what time requires, not in where eternity belongs. What relates to time, however far beyond it, must undertake its temporal condition and this must be the case in whatever terms of verbal text or verbal personhood or other human cognisance we think that relating has devised.

The located and the dated opening of revealing drama, one then turning to register its close, will – on divine part – be no forfeiture of the conti-nuities of its before and after. These abide both in the integrity of the great, unchanged Original and in treasured import of the presentation made. It was precisely these time-told things in their quality as eternal that designed the 'theatre' as the realm of their 'beholding'. They were safe in the dramatic will that had their sequences in trust. The 'there' and 'thus' of their stage could be memoried anywhere.

Advent and ascension, the coming and the leaving, the prelude and the climax of such *incarnatus est* would be the physical history serving as the given disclosure of the divine nature *vis-à-vis* the character and the expectation of the created order where we humans are. What technical Christian theology thinks a pre-existent and a post-existent Christ are the eternal fidelities in God to which faith witnesses. How in the one case the Virgin Birth and, in the other, resurrection and ascension, sig-nify the temporal/eternal we must take up in Chapters Three and Four. The one must be seen and known as the time-conceived initiative, the other as the time-bequeathed completeness and perpetuation. Each belongs with the sovereignty for ever the original and the inclusive Lord, the Alpha and the Omega of the eternal mind. This 'Word made flesh', in time-employing physicality, is Biblically told in the imagery of a journeying story that is, via the Gospels, a storied journey. The travelling – which is a travailing – analogy is physically described but as never merely physical. Its spiritual 'sent-on-its-way-ness' has to do with how we humans are in time and place which must be entered if we are to be divinely taught and loved.

Physicality there had to be. Concerting birth and 'learning' death were the 'wayfaring' necessitated by condescension to the human task. These – as we must further study – are what Christian faith has meant to acknowledge in the veneration of Mary in the temper of her own Magnificat and to recognise in the farewelling of the disciples on 'the holy mount'. The spiritual, never compromised or abandoned in the physical whereby it was authentically itself, issued from the eternity where it ever reigned and thither returned in re-assuming the glory whence it came.

In thinking of a river it is idle to enquire to which of the banks it owes itself in flowing through them. For it has made them what they are in being the entity it is – the entity whose being they fulfil. So it is with 'Him made man for our redemption'. *Incarnatus est* tells a divine 'more likest God in being born', a divine necessarily among us in being ever beyond and over us, eternally reciprocal to our humanity.

'God stooping shows sufficient of His light' was how Robert Browning told this comprehension of the Incarnation. The coming and the going through an incidence of years are the signal occasion of divine venture and active grace. Only stage and acts, as Shakespeare's Chorus knew, 'admit gentles all' unto 'the swelling scene'. As then so now, it is 'Our thoughts' that must duly 'deck' those scenes made present to our love.

'Time's sacrament', then, is apt for this perceived meaning of *incarnatus est*, as Christian faith confesses it. We can defer to Chapter Six all the disputanda which contest it on whatever ground. 'Sacrament' was always the word that had to do with meaning not merely denoted, but transacted in the act that told it. It always recruited the physical in the having of the spiritual. It happens as a given and a received. It is multiplied everywhere in daily life, in the shaking of a hand or the exchanging of a kiss. These – as it were – 'eventuate' relationship. An embrace is never unilateral, nor a ritual ablution performed unawares. An extended hand will always be a sign – significantly grasped or significantly refused. Flowers do not convey their freight of sympathy until they are admired. Our being 'met in His Name' was always Jesus' proviso about His being 'in the midst'. Faith consists in identifying where its attraction summons it, namely where a deed or history with that intent has placed it to await a sealing recognition. We recall the poet met in Chapter One who pondered:

Now might this goodness draw our souls above
Which drew down God in such attractive love.

Sacraments can well be understood as a kind of progression from the
role of metaphor – as precisely happens when there is 'the word made
flesh'. It is, therefore, sound proceeding, to come to them for theology as
one might in the art of literary criticism. What a word can achieve on the
ear, sacrament can bestow on the eye. Either conveys the significance of
things, the one heard, the other done. The porter in *Macbeth* conjures up
his several meanings from 'the knocking at the gate', not merely as of a
sound he heard but from an event that woke him out of drunken sleep.
Verbal sense has storied shape and the work of a told fiction graduates
into an actual history. Then, for example, an exodus can have the sacramental quality that contains and tells a destiny.

Sacraments work by alerting to query – what might this mean? – so that
inattention is turned round into deliberation. They prompt the kind of
register that will take stock – be it swift or slow – and understand. Such
move from metaphor to sacrament, from words to acts, turns what James
Joyce called 'the referential nature of words' into the operation of will.
We move from a reference that is mental to one that is feasible and performative. Oftentimes they combine as when, either way, we speak, for
example, of 'truth dawning' or of 'lips sealed'. Then even as words are
'playing a part', so too must we.

Defining 'the Christian Jesus' as time's sacrament means there was an
'eventuation' for 'our knowledge of the love of God', thus brought into
our ken. Like language in its yield of metaphor, so event in its presentation of sacrament serves for intimation and disclosure. It awaits the
greeting of the spirit it was intended to evoke, a greeting which
'constructs' that intent and need not be suspect or dubious in doing so,
since it has found a mutuality in an inter-confirmation. The nature of
Christian faith has always been that way, as is evident from the very shape
of its New Testament literature as being *of* and *from* their theme, the faith
of Jesus known in the faith about Him.

But can it really be that the Eternal, according to this faith, has made,
is making, in human time to human hearts the sort of gesture for response
that sacraments of ours perform, as the ring in marriage or the presentation of a key as the warrant for entry into office? We do the supreme
sacramental dimension wrong by comparisons in this demeaning way,
except that there are none that could be worthy and truths may pass
through lowly doors. Can 'God in Christ' as time's sacrament indeed
mean that we have the frame in which all else must be set, whether for
our intellectual assurance or for our practice of living?

[34]

If so, are we being determined by that which is a determination of our own? Have not the 'de-constructionists' insisted – as we must address them in Chapter Six – that no faith, or system, or religious commitment can be other than entirely relative and, therefore, never inclusively valid, still less relied on absolutely in the way that 'all time's sacrament' proposes? No sacraments avail except for those who will to find them such. Maybe in our sense of the Incarnation and of this Christian Jesus we are only, and wilfully, self-deceived? In any event, can any specific time be the sacrament of all time?

Certainly *not* for 'all time', if, in time, we are including those faiths which see it only as transience and not as history. Only in significant history with historical register does time really transpire as humanly lived and known. Only so could experience it yields be detected and greeted as sacramental. What is undergone as mere duration being less than human time, could present no arresting tokens as to where its surest secret lay. Time's sacrament, in Christian or any other sense, can only have the human realm in mind. For theology moves and means within what some have called 'anthropic' range so that the reality of God – far from being comprehended as only real within that realm – is not comprehensible outside. 'In Him we live and move and have our being'; 'there of Him we have our knowledge'.

It was bold of Alice Meynell (1847–1922) around a century ago to set 'His dealings' with us, 'abiding' in

> The signal to a maid, the human birth,
> The lesson, and the young man crucified.

And then to wonder how 'He trod the Pleiades, the Lyre, the Bear' – bold but also deviant, enquiring for 'the million forms of God those stars unroll'. Some mysterious mutuality between God and humankind under-lies the very principle of the Incarnation. As she rightly had it 'no other planet knows the secret of His way with us'. 'Our race' have not merely 'kept their Lord's entrusted Word', the destiny to be entrusted made us the race we are – a situation gathered into why the 'entrusted Word' would be incarnate in our very flesh.

Thus time's sacrament places outside our anxiety all those aeons of unimaginable time-dimension, those immense vastnesses of spatial universe because, in the privilege of our human-ness, it absorbs them. Theology takes note of cosmology as where intelligible history transpires and where, only so, we humankind belong. 'The Word is made flesh.' We cannot look for the sacramental where its possibilities do not exist.

It is, therefore, due awe and not some case arguing our own vulgarity as mortals, which we must draw from awareness of how enormous is the setting of our terrestrial habitat. Is it not precisely the knowledge, humanly reached, of how totally dwarfing of us those infinite spaces are which constitutes our humankind sole monitor of the awesomeness of which they are unaware? Immensities of cosmic measure only have spiritual reckoning in the cognisance of the otherwise infinitesimal. Again, even in the vast abyss of space and time, 'the Word is made flesh', inasmuch that only 'the flesh' is word-able. The universe has waited to be told its age, staying long eternally unaware. Humankind, spectating, give meaning to the spectacle. Fearful souls should not let timidity unnerve their theology since even daunting things are latent with sacramental meaning on every hand, by dint of human reckoning with their perceived significance. The vast spaces, their ageless time, are not some 'great wink of eternity' if we read aright our homing earth. With due imagination, nature via senses and the landscape will always carry us towards the sacramental and poetry draw us on.

How much more so then could history yield sacramental significance, at least for those minded to be alert to its plea for comprehension and interpretation? For it is natural history, seasons, flora and fauna, tides and shores, phenomena on every hand, that house political history, the hither and thither of societies and states. If earth-experience in the human soul compels all contemplation of vastnesses around it into the utmost local confining to one globe of the clues by which it may be read, might not earth's history also find its defining index no less narrowly identified where we might say of it: *incarnatus est*? Any such theological confidence that 'here is where' about a personality in a context would be analogous to cosmology happy to be of necessity terrestrial in taking in 'the infinite spaces'.

Astro-physics would have many reasons for not pressing the analogy too far and so, indeed, would a wise Christology. Yet the human world is, for us humans, the working clue we cannot refuse to the universe we register around it, so within that enabling habitat of conscious history faith might think to find where the key to significance was placed, and placed no less conclusively.

That 'the Christian Jesus' is a verdict made from a history read is freely acknowledged. As 'Disputanda' must later explore, it is a 'construct' that many have willed to deconstruct. Chapters Three and Four to follow will recognize and examine how New Testament faith was, like all history, a story told out of a story needing telling and how New Testament documentation could have come into existence in no other way. For it bears all the marks of being wanted by community because community had been wanted in its meaning. 'That which we have seen and heard and handled' was derived from them as text because they were derived from it. There was everything mutual between things textual and ecclesiastical. Narrative came out of conviction, the spur of either to the other. It was not witness from neutrality. Witness from neutrality is a contradiction in terms. The diary of one's wedding day is likely to contain some bias with much bliss.

Yet this situation, so evident in 'the Christian Jesus' – and thus, for many, so suspect – belongs in some measure to all history. Historiography is currently at odds with itself as to how 'scientific' historians can hope to be, how in jeopardy about the usages of language, how confident around what some have called 'the fetish of sources'. These doubts which accompany us everywhere make it the more precarious to locate in human history anything so inclusive as to be the sacrament of the Eternal where all assurance dwells.

Nevertheless, the impulse to look for one, to ponder where and how it might locate, is surely present in the will for history at all. The historian, even in the endless particulars, is on quest for clues, for factors that might clarify into evidences of where meaning resides. Such, we might say, is the sacramental instinct, not merely to think ourselves significant but to appreciate how and where and when, supremely, it is so, through

> The power of human minds,
> To men as they are men within themselves.
> How oft high service is performed within . . .
> . . . men for contemplation framed
> . . . unpractised in the strife of phrase . . .
> Whose very soul perhaps would sink
> Beneath them, summoned to such intercourse,
> The thought, the image and the silent joy:
> Words are but under agents in their souls.

So Wordsworth, in the 1835 'Postscript' to his published poetry.

That time, duly registered and undergone, is capable of yielding to our human-ness the secret of ourselves as time-positioned is the crux of religion, even as it is also of the ultimate irreligion that distrusts any such yielding. The differences between the great faiths turn, in large measure, on where they find their inclusive sacrament, what in Hebraic idiom could be 'the place of the Name', where all came to a mediated certitude with words no more than 'under agents'.

In that Jewish tradition it was the lived history of their own people-hood, its fabled ancestry in nomadism, its defining emancipation in Exodus, its land and memory marriage, its exile and return, its dependable survival through diaspora. These were all elements of 'truth-placing', an enduring awareness of identity, Yahweh's and their own as Yahweh's 'people'. 'Summoned to such intercourse' they transacted the very experience of destiny both told and lived in that story. They became, in turn, 'the people of the Book' that housed it, even as 'the Book' could 'house it' because they were its people.

It was, we may assume, this famous phrase about Jewry – which pointedly the Islamic Qur'an employs – that weighed on Islam's own reception of sacramental history, only that the 'book' category shifts from a *tanakh* text *about* events and becomes itself the event as the text *per se*, its mediation on to Muhammad's lips and its arrival by faithful recitation into inscribed pages.

Writers, in mundane idiom, have sometimes dreamed of writing the book that would fulfil all books and be the ultimate achievement of that art. This, in God-given terms, the Qur'an purports to be, as 'sealing' all due prophethoods as these belonged through all the antecedent centuries before their Arabic culmination in Muhammad's text. That could obtain, however, because it was not Muhammad's authored text but the one that became his by heavenly mediation to his utterance in the phenomenon of *wahy*, namely revelation-in-inspiration as one reality, divinely granted and humanly undergone.

There is, then, a double sacrament as Islam believes, whereby identified history has come to possess the ultimate divine speech. Time has contained what educates all time. This becomes in turn a sacrament of private recitation in which this 'very word(s) of Allah' is personally read from the page, recited in utterance and stored in memory. Thus the believer 'partakes' of what is God's in the most intimate fashion, recruiting those very organs by which humans are articulate in vocal and mental terms. That capability comes about because, by divine mercy, this memorable 'Book' exists on earth – memorably in every sense as at once eternal, present, legible and recited. The years of its *tanzil*, or 'sending down', are the point in history where its arrival encompassed our human education – education, in turn, being the shape of Allah's relation to our mortal time and place, the 'sign' that 'signifies'.

Muslims may not immediately approve or use the sacramental term, exclusers as they are of 'priesthood' as they read it in Christianity. Even so, there is extended sacrament drawn from the supremely Quranic one, in that the Mecca of its main incidence becomes the focus of communal Muslim pilgrimage where the content, and the deep solidarity, of the pilgrim ritual renews participation in the meaning. Likewise the calendar of years dates from the mid-point in its incidence, while the mosque has its vital liturgical direction on that *qiblah* to Mecca. These, and other, aspects of Islamic Din, or religious practice, bind believing piety into the defining ministry Qur'an possession and recitation have to the Muslim soul. Their reception of time's sacrament so identified, avails to the defining of themselves. Somehow the meaning of all time can be read at one time and thence suffuse all ensuing time, even as it has climaxed all preceding time.

Even the utmost scepticism will not escape the need to sacramentalise its negativity. Samuel Beckett's vivid reduction of dramatic action to something like the silence of a lived grave serves, in its canny way, to denote the human condition and invite its audience, at a (contrived) loss, to know it so. Beckett's Vladimir and Estragon 'wait for a Godot who never comes'. 'Let's go' is said where neither moves. Even vacuity will somehow symbolise itself and become a transaction of palpable emptiness. Examples are legion of this technique of a futility that is in no way abstract, at once endured and unendurable. Even pointlessness will need its images.

Looking affirmatively for 'time's sacrament', what need the criteria to be? The New Testament, responsive to where it found surest reason to find it, identified its 'Lord Jesus Christ' as where criteria were best satisfied. It had the same instinct of 'looking to God', holding like Jews and – later – Muslims a confident theism that could rely on God significant for the world and a world significant to God. It differed from both in finding the Judaic too limited in human range and the Islamic too reliant on the success of law and tuition alone as sufficing the divine obligation to our human predicament. The Judaic did not see that obligation as indiscriminating and inclusive but rather selective in the ethnic terms of unilateral covenant and a singular exodus. The Islamic, for its part, did not see the divine Lawgiver truly engaged in the failing or short-falling of all law in making actual the good it willed and enjoined.

If, in either case, any notion of divine obligation towards the human scene were to be thought improper to their theism, there could be no logic in that scruple. Obligation, in either case, is deeply there. Judaic covenant believes deeply in the liability of God to keep it and, indeed, to initiate it. Only so could it be mandatory on Him. As for Islam, Surah 4.165 notes that had Allah *not* sent 'messengers, warners, news-bringers' to humanity, He would have been in default as God. There would have been a human 'case against Him'. For, in the absence of the prophets, humankind would have been left in *Jahiliyyah*, or 'ignorance' – a condition which would have frustrated the whole business of our creaturehood as ever a divine enterprise.

The Christian sense of 'God in Christ', of 'Mary's babe' and 'the risen Lord' and all between, with the Cross the crux – these are the apt elements in its intellectual love of God. For an intellectual love there needs to be if we are what theists need to become. Such love perceives an inclusivity of range as inherently proper to divine Lordship, anticipated as it might historically be by some who thought it private to themselves. Anticipation would not rightly be such if not duly realised in a destiny into universal reach.

Likewise redemption, as a divine corollary to legislation, will be seen as 'loving God with all our mind'. For the good intent of law, as monitoring a good creation in the deliberate custody of human creaturehood, is not attained by law alone. Our human capacity to flout its good intent is evident enough. Law's own duty by that good intent – in being law at all – argues a need within it to retrieve, by means beyond law's own retributive competence, what law had sought of righteousness and truth. Unless law acquiesces in lawlessness, returning all to chaos and futility, betraying the good it has in care, it must, for its own sake, recruit what it cannot itself deploy, namely the grace that forgives via the love that redeems. It must do so in line with its own moral integrity.

All this is within a duly intellectual love of God. The Incarnation has to be seen as the ultimate logic of theism, an incarnation, moreover, that contains the dimensions only measured by something like the Cross of Christ. Far from being, in popular parlance, some 'myth of God incarnate', it has to be seen as the only theology sufficiently answerable both to the credible trustworthiness of a good creation and a sane and sober realism about humankind.

We put that case another way if we reckon duly with the significance in Jesus teaching and Jesus suffering as integral to each other. They are precisely the elements which much scholarship has wanted to separate. Yet that 'Ecce homo' Pilate used to hail one he saw as a tragic figure belongs no less with that same itinerant in Galilee. Indeed, one eminent 19th century historian, J. R. Seeley, used the words as title for a notable study of the ethical teaching of Jesus, where 'no heart is pure that is not passionate, no virtue is safe that is not enthusiastic'.

The Gospels found time's sacrament in both aspects of Jesus and in their unison. Incarnation faith saw no wedge between them. Jesus taught as he suffered, suffered as he taught. Each had its part in the other. Law, which in precept and commandment seems so often academic and prosaic, even intimidating, became in him a personified attraction, appealing by the force of character and the enlistment of hope and aspiration. Those Beatitudes were heartening statements of fact and not merely encodings of duty. The meaning of 'the Word made flesh' was a profoundly ethical reality, whereby 'the moral law within' of philosophy could be known as 'categorical' by dint of being lived in a ministry of due fulfilment in the here-and-now of human being.

So much faith in the Incarnation had always meant to say. The burden

of its witness was a theology which, though it would need to become articulate in careful creed, had originated in a life. It would duly be scriptured
in something like biography – biography in Gospel form suited to that
task. Both Scripture and creed would be the intellectual love of the God
identified as 'the most moved Mover', whose nature not only required
their witness but had drawn it forth. This birth of faith was cradled in the
birth of Christ.

So too was it brought to full dimension in his death. For what ensued
in the climax of his suffering, in sequel to his preaching, told only too
darkly the unwantedness of its content in our sort of world. The stark
reality is this non-success of Jesus' word as precept and example. He was
not the traditional rabbi, surrounded by a coterie of custodians perpetuating his legal legacy. Those Beatitudes came to their Gethsemane. 'Let
him be crucified' was delayed comment on the Sermon on the Mount –
delayed indeed, but the more telling thereby. The content, we might say,
of Jesus' teaching was made shipwreck on the issue of his authority. That
authority, though popularly loved and liberating, was disallowed by pride
of religion and the obtuseness of collective sin.

Thus no faith, sprung from a Jesus of the Cross, could ever be sanguine
about human amenability to law, or human perfectibility by precept and
injunction. Time's sacrament, if – on Christian ground – it were ever to
avail as such, would need to have shape in a history honestly realist about
the human world. It is that very quality faith, fashioned at the Cross – at
the Cross in its eventuation out of Bethlehem – knew itself to have
attained, and attained thanks alone to the story where the secret lay. Thus
it had particular date and place only in being a universal epitome.

Epitome of what? – of 'the sin of the world', indeed, but not only so. It
had 'in flesh' what alone redeems. It was seen as transacting the forgive-
ness sin always needs, if its guilt is to be overcome and its weight borne.
In relation to the death of Jesus, the prime question has always been: How
crucified? not Who crucified? The 'who' question was always incidental.
The 'how' belonged with sinful human nature, inseparable from the 'how'
of Jesus' bearing it. The sceptic, as we must later note, may always say
that we have no sure evidence about those 'words from the Cross', only
that they are far less credible as invented or imagined than in their authenticity.

'Father, forgive them . . .' 'This day with me . . .' 'Father, into Thy
hands . . .' and others in the retrospect of 'Why didst Thou forsake me?'
told the 'bearing' that was always physical in its undergirding by what
was always the soul of being Messianic. Only what is 'not overcome of
evil' attains to 'overcome evil with good'. Such was the sacrament in
history of Jesus crucified.

It has to be said that its recognition has been badly served by the 'lamb imagery' that lay to hand from old tradition drawn from Temple sacrifice whose altar immolations could never remotely measure what the Cross was to Jesus. What, in the animal realm, was ever involuntary and merely ritually inflicted could never begin to register the dark of a Gethsemane, the agony of a Calvary. Only these could use the human cry: 'The cup my Father gives me . . .' or 'If it may not pass . . .' The Cross, therefore, has to be rescued from much reductionism of its mystery by analogies that fail its real dimensions. This 'Lamb of God' was not of that far-off order of endlessly repeated acts of sacrifice, of holocaust only fictitiously vicarious.

Happily, that Levitical 'lamb language' points where it truly serves, as when, for example, Jeremiah compares the travail of his ministry as of one 'led like a lamb or an ox to the slaughter' (11:19). His imagery – and indeed his experience – recur still more pointedly in the 'songs of the servant', notably Isaiah 53:6. Here, at one but vital remove, the 'lamb language' offers itself for New Testament borrowing in John 1:29, and the Letter to the Hebrews. No trace of artificial substitution remains. Instead there is the deep truth of ultimate prophethood as a suffering to tell, and a telling in suffering. Such was pre-eminently the lot of Jeremiah, bearing for some forty years the burden of an unrelenting role he could neither endure nor renounce. What he suffered was inherent in who he was divinely required to be. The Wisdom of Solomon (chapter 2) has a later, but comparable, portrait of a 'man of sorrows' as made so in being a 'man with the word'.

We have to understand a fidelity that is all of one piece. Ministry with truth incurs hostility. The task holds on in loyalty. Antipathy increases. The encounter lengthens. Travail deepens and, inexorably, bearing the truth means bearing the cost. The person of the prophet becomes a hostage to the theme he tells. It is one he will not deny by silence. By his calling he has no option to resign it. Only so is he 'just', honest, true and faithful. Only so, too, the verdict: 'The just lives by his faithfulness' and so too, lives the faith he tells. It does not succumb because he does not falter. It abides undiminished because he abides undaunted by what would extinguish its meaning. The travail of his fidelity is the triumph of his Lord. For only in and with his Lord was his fidelity sustained. There has been a divine/human partnership in a discernible redemption.

Here, in this prophetic precedent providing the Messianic frame of reference, we can trace how New Testament faith came to its supreme formula of 'the Lamb of God' and of 'God in Christ', and so in turn the centuries could recognise in what they told as time's sacrament of grace.

Messianic expectation had a long, if contentious, history. It was rooted in belief in a good and responsible creation. It constituted the shape of hope in divine fidelity, the answer there must be – if God is God – to humankind as historically proved to be, in exile, guilt and wrong done and undergone. It had precedent in the past of exodus as when Nehemiah pointedly said of God: 'You won a reputation that day' (9:10). What, into further future, must that 'reputation' hold and how would it be made good and evident?

That time might duly have its 'sacrament of ripe fulfilment' was a yearning latent in the tradition of prophetic 'vision' 'sealed for a time to come' (Isaiah 8:16 and 29:11–12). Hope is always of that order, in line with the normal, legal pattern of 'sealing' documents and deeds. These, by definition, have to do with a 'becoming past' that 'reaches into a certain future', which is only 'certain' in the conclusive sense the text holds for it because it would, otherwise, be totally 'uncertain'. So much in Hebraic prophethood was of this order, only being loyal in being anticipatory. 'For the time to come' would learn to say, as the apostles did: 'But now . . .' or: 'This is that of which the prophets told'.

'Sealed among my disciples,' Isaiah 8:16 had said: no heritage without heirs. Anticipation cannot be contemporary with fulfilment but time's sacrament may be recognised when all generations can belong, as Mary sang – belong because its meaning unites them. Here we meet the supreme paradox that the faith as to 'God in Christ' did not do so. The Messianic realisation, from which the New Testament derived, heirs of Isaiah and Jeremiah did not share, though such heirs were also its defining percipients. Aspects of that situation belong with Chapter Six. The tragic tensions that ensued from it, however, did not undo the Jew/non-Jew unison in the birth of Christianity. New Testament faith only existed in seeing itself heir to anticipations by which its people knew themselves defined and warranted.

It was, therefore, poetically right that what we are seeing in 'the Christian Jesus' as time's sacrament itself required and yielded personal sacraments sealing discipleship in its truth. They were baptism and the Holy Communion. What history held for its comprehension the answering self would hold for its anchorage of mind, its discourse in society and its hallowing of heart. Perhaps we might say, in musical terms, that the 'score' through which, in divine Incarnation, we read the meaning of our humanity, we must find what, as instrumentalists, calls also for ourselves. There was this quality entirely apposite about 'the Word made flesh' in having prerogative rights over our discipleship as, analogously, its dwelling-place. So would Mary discover, as the following chapter will explore. The inclusive sacrament from eternity to human time would be consistent with itself in sacramentalising its recognition in the human heart.

This it did in 'bread and wine'. Those disciples with whom its future lay, since an 'ending beyond an imminent end' lay ahead in the Passion and the parting, were gathered round their Master. The awe of ancient 'Passover' was in the air. A dire sense of impending crisis weighed on uncomprehending spirits. Jesus said, taking bread and wine: 'Do this in remembrance of me.' Did the words fall bitterly on their ears – not only for how ominous they were but, more, for the crushing implication they would one day be forgetting him?

The point is central to both sacraments, to Incarnation and Communion alike. For, plainly, Jesus – for the disciples – was unforgettable. Could they have lived as one those brief and crowded years, with such memorable scenes, such deep occasions, and ever fail to hold them in their memory? It cannot be that bread and wine comprised a ritual designed to stave off oblivion. Nor could they be a device somehow to perpetuate a trace that, otherwise, passed out of the business of living.

It was not 'whether' but 'how' about 'remembrance' that 'this table' had to do and 'how' in two orders of intent, the one where the focus lay; the other the inner demand inseparable from all continuity. Time's sacrament in this Christ would have its future in ever vital sacramental form and never in mere recollection or idle admiration. Sacraments are always meant to be performative both as to why they signify and how they motivate.

It is noteworthy that, on 'the night in which he was betrayed', Jesus did not suggest some ceremonial – say annual reading of his Sermon on the Mount or other collection of sayings and parables. That might have been appropriate had teaching been his only *métier*. Even so, it would only have elicited admiration with a repute comparable to that of Socrates or perhaps the eager applause that greeted Demosthemes or Cicero – essentially a possessive, self-congratulating esteem that held no sanction on obedience.

No. We have to say, in a paradox like Kierkegaard's, that 'Jesus did not come to be admired'. He came to be followed – and followed – supremely – in his Passion. There emphatically, he focused his sacramental *anamnesis* in 'bread and wine'. 'Do this . . .' 'Make this your own . . .' would tell where the climax of the Incarnation lay and what it must entail in discipled answer to its comprehension. Ceremonial audition would merely leave us in an approbation that might well recoil patronisingly upon ourselves in having such an eikon. Only Communion in the tokens of the Passion would find us honestly recalling it.

For recalling through it would mean that intensely personal business of 'eating and drinking' – no cannibalism as has been crudely alleged – but the aptest of symbols concerning the nature of faith as somehow analogous to the body's metabolism in finding its very health in its food reception. 'Taste and see' was no idle metaphor of the psalmist: it is rather the steady secret of food into life, of life via food. It is of the nature of faith to make our own what is ours in Christ and, as faith is, so are eating and drinking, namely inalienable – an activity for which there can be no substitute, in which no substitute avails.

On both counts, the elements in Holy Communion are of this order but, by the same token, like all hospitality, are inherently communal. 'Take this . . . among yourselves' uses a plural verb. The essential personalism of true faith obtains only in its incorporation into fellowship. There is no 'loneliness of the long distance runner', scattered as the apostolic Church became. The one Eucharist cemented the solidarity it created among them. The 'I' and 'we' of their society were found in the one unity discerning, in the double sense, 'the Lord's body'.

That was a telling occasion and a pregnant word in 1 Corinthians 11, when still immature Christians misconstrued their 'holy communion' as an ordinary meal where they might follow vulgar habits of a free-for-all in what was duly an 'each-in-all'. They did not 'discern' the sacramental 'body' via the 'bread and wine' seeing that they did not 'discern' the pattern and the onus of their unity in coming to it. They were one in that in which their oneness lay.

It is this extension of the word 'the body' from the one Incarnation of 'the Word made flesh' to the Church as its shaping into faith and love that indicates how time's sacrament enjoys its future. The ascension of the Lord, which is its earthly 'curtain' (to recall our earlier analogy) on the unchanging divine significance it carried, has earthly ongoing in the community which becomes thereby 'his body' in that 'absence'. It is 'his body' informed and enabled by 'the Holy Spirit', who – like the inner principle of the Incarnation – requires the human means. The Fourth Gospel takes up this 'Church which is his body' theme via the imagery of the Temple, as 'the place of the divine Name', the rendezvous where Yahweh could be encountered as where He had willed encounter might be. That Temple was the fulfilment – the city-wise of 'the tent of the Presence' from the years of nomadism and the centuries prior to its building. It had been, in geographical and ritual terms, itself a sort of 'sacrament' joining locale to experience.

Likewise, in its fullest terms the *Ave atque Vale* of 'the Christian Jesus', the advent and the ascension that held the Incarnation, were our meeting with 'the glory in the bosom of the Father'.

The sacrament of 'bread and wine' deriving from time's sacrament in Christ had its other counter-partnering sacrament in baptism. The word was used, according to Luke, by Jesus, in anticipation of his Passion

(12:50) while Matthew has him asking disciples whether they can think to share it (20:22–23). Ensuing Christian baptism, like the Eucharist, excludes all nodding, patronising association with the Lord. It means carrying the 'Christian' name as enlisting the identity it then denotes.

Paul saw in the event of 'Jesus as the Christ' the patterned elements of discipleship – a learning in his school, a taking of his yoke, a marking by his wounds – the last in the sense of being drawn personally into a self-hood they had educated. 'He died for all that they who live should live no longer to themselves but as His who died for them'. (2 Corinthians 5:14–15). In this he was one with his Lord's own saying about 'losing life to find it'. The self should count itself 'crucified with Christ', counting thus 'dead', the old, the natural, the self-indulging persona, to receive it again, new-made in Christ. This he called 'being conformed to Christ's death' so that 'the power of the resurrection' might encompass 'newness of being', brought to pass, in the old, now new, selfhood.

This reading of the Lord's Passion, as at once an event in the world and a sustained crisis in the personal disciple, fulfilled the sacramental principle of meaning that was ever performative – in the one case of time-long divine disclosure, in the other of human participation truly realised in personal life. The Christ formed in our likeness would have his likeness formed in us – the one a sure theology in wonder, the other the 'liberty of perfect freedom'.

Motherhood being requisite to Incarnation, 'Mary with Magnificat' must be the preface to those 'likenesses', as instrumental to the one, as symbol to the other.

CHAPTER THREE

Mary with Magnificat

To think and write about 'the Christian Jesus' is the surest context in which to have the measure of Mary's celebratory Song and why the evangelist Luke set it on her lips. For it was his perception that adapted it from other sources into his 'Infancy Gospel'. 'The low estate of his hand-maiden' was a shape of words capable of several interpretations only to be rightly discerned in the ensuing career of the child she bore.

Time's sacrament, as studied in the previous chapter, certainly required a natal point seeing that only in birth can a life begin. Faith in 'incarnation' could have no other way. Eternal initiative – if such it be – will need temporal initiation. The Christianity of the New Testament firmly excluded any time-origin post-dating human wombing. As Richard Crashaw had it, 'the eternal word' being once 'unable to speak a word' was crucial to the stature the speaking years of word and deed and wound would at length fulfil. Motherhood would be implicit in the eternal enterprise for its own completeness' sake so that the human factor, in its perennial necessity, was recruited into partnership. 'Regarding low estate,' as Luke has us realise, was not only the human necessity of nativity: it was the divine poetry in the telling of it. 'The travail of Mary's low estate' was enlisted as the prerogative of the kind of love the Incarnation holds. The beginning of time's sacrament would advertise its character.

But we only truly reach the significance of Mary via the Jesus whose relevance was gathered into the version of him that gave life and form to apostolic Christianity. The latter is the conclusive 'conception by the Holy Spirit' to which the former was no more than the birth-inaugural. Natally, doubtless, we have Jesus thanks to Mary: essentially we only have Mary thanks to Jesus. Is it not somehow always so in the biographies of history? Pregnancy contrived us all. Incarnation, if we can receive its meaning, shares that mystery.

It is, however, only the sequel that discovers, discloses and describes what inauguration held in hand. Birth that is ever prospective of life is always comprehended from life's retrospect. It is important for readers of the Gospels and users of the Creed to make the effort of mind to think into the biographical sequence of the faith which must begin with the adult Jesus. For it was only this which lent ultimate interest to the vital nativity from which it had derived. We must begin with Mark and his 'Jesus came preaching' or, antecedently – as indeed does Mark also – with that abrupt insertion, at John 1:6, where the writer breaks into his sublime theology of 'the Word made flesh' with the calm, prosaic announcement: 'There was a man sent from God whose name was John.'

That was an annunciation which came only years later than Mary's but in being its sequel was about its *raison d'être*. John, as the renewer of the long dormant tradition of divine 'messengers', served to inaugurate the preaching ministry of Jesus in the Messianic inclusiveness where Mary had found her destiny in the other, necessary, role of inauguration that birth fulfils. Traditional faith, after the pattern of Matthew and Luke, tells hers first only because, as with Mark and John, the ultimate primacy was in the sequel. Even in day-to-day history how else do birth-places become items of interest and enquiry, inasmuch as

> What greatly is done by prophet or poet,
> By scholar or king, is a womb-cradled thing?

Only then is the instrumental motherhood saluted in the gratitude of debt and reverence.

Faith, therefore, needs to take its Christmas from the perceptions of its Gethsemane and of all that intervened to fashion the acknowledgement, in Jesus, of 'the Christ of God'. The case becomes the more clear when we appreciate how many of the features of the Christmas story have their origin from that Christhood, realised and confessed by disciples only at the end of the story. For many of them derived from Messianic association and were only seen to be apposite because Jesus, in ministry 'even unto death', as faith read him, had warranted their application. The fact that, otherwise, some of these attributions would seem far-fetched or elusive only makes more obvious the impulse to their fascination.

Do we, for example, owe the sentiment of so many loved carols and how 'Ox and ass before him bow' to a wistful exegesis of Isaiah 1:3: 'The ox knows his owner and the ass his master's crib'? Was it from this strange ingenuity that 'the crib' figures so readily in the lore of the Nativity? For ingenuity there was – so evident that the whole relation of text to meaning, of its intention to reader, is at stake. Yet many ancient texts, Biblical or otherwise, were subject to such imaginative verdicts where 'intention' was as likely to be willed on it as drawn from it. In the context of Isaiah 1:3, the words pointedly contrast the docility of domesticated beasts with the obduracy of wilful humans.

'Only simple shepherds knew that God had sent His Son', sang the music of Noel, but did they – in those deeply theological terms? Clearly they had no conscious share in the Johannine mind nor could they have understood the Prologue when it came to wording. Yet once we have taken in the Messianic – still then future – what more congruent than shepherds with their flocks? 'Sharon shall be a fold of flocks' cried the Isaiah of 65:10, when 'seed out of Jacob and out of Judah an inheritor of my mountains' was announced. The imagery of the shepherd was deep in the Messianic tradition, for example of Isaiah 40:11: 'He shall feed his flock like a shepherd . . .' If, in those fields of Bethlehem, they were guarding the lambs of adjacent Temple sacrifice – where the daily altar holocaust required a heavy toll – the aptness of their 'Let us go and see' is the more clear.

All, however, turns on the faith-to-be about the child born. Given that fact, still then waiting its hidden disclosure, the whole poetry, whether of prophet or carol, is duly in place. It may well be that the whole structure of Nativity narrative – and indeed of the Passion history – belongs with the perception, as being there fulfilled, of hints and musings discernibly ready for the unsuspected anticipations of which ultimate history had made them possessed.

So did the Magi really travel 'all that way' because Isaiah had cried: 'The Gentiles shall come to thy light and kings to the brightness of thy rising' (60:30)? The story of 'the star' might rightly be explored in astronomical record and have its place in proof of historicity but the final credenda of the Matthean narrative must belong with 'the Christian Jesus' we are tracing. 'A cold coming they had of it' is then authentic within the idiom of faith perception, as poetry ever is to the wonder in the heart.

The devotion of Matthew's Gospel to the citation of scriptural precedent is eloquent enough of his editorial intention – so far so that his reference to Jesus being 'called a Nazarene' seems to have no origin. Basic, it would seem, to his purpose was a double motive – to ground the witness to Jesus as the Christ with the utmost deference to what might persuade fellow Jews of its veracity and the vital ground of Messianic actuality as faith held it to be.

Do we then owe the location of the nativity in Bethlehem solely to the lineage of David and the expectation of Micah 5:2? Does mere historicity matter, insofar as scholars may wish to think the location wrong? Will the case be susceptible of resolution by research into the dating of 'the census' and/or local officialdom? For all so minded, Yes. Essentially, however, the Messianic actuality faith confesses will not be thereby the more true nor the less assured depending on the academic verdict. For Matthew's witness to location belongs firmly within his perception of

Jesus and he is writing out of years of communal confidence in that perception. If historians wish to fault him they must needs go to the heart of his assurance which alone carries with it the incidentals.

How dearly Coptic Christianity has cherished the narrative of the sojourn in Egypt. Do they owe it merely to Hosea's reference – for such it was – to the Exodus in his 'Out of Egypt have I called my son' (11:1). Is Jeremiah 31:15 responsible for the massacre of the innocents? Manifestly not, in either case. For Hosea's thought on the Exodus belonged with his agonising pleas to his own generation concerning their apostasy to the meaning of their history, while Jeremiah was both sharing and drying the tragic tears of his generation in the anguish of their common day. The Gospel according to Matthew knew well how Herod was that sort of king. Again it is the Messianic secret proleptic in the infancy of Jesus that prompts him to inter-associate event and memory fit to underline each other.

But if these, and other, points of poetic interpretation, however seemingly wilful, can be contained within the validity of Jesus Christianly understood, the same is not true of that other and most crucial borrowing from Isaiah, namely the passage about a nativity in 7:14. There, the given context will not sustain the doctrine of 'the virgin birth' of Jesus, nor would it afford any poetic warrant – other passages did – to read the two nativities in question in any over-lapping terms.

There is a clear and unambiguous context in Isaiah 7 where a mother's being a 'virgin' is quite extraneous to the meaning of that 'Immanuel'. On the contrary, the logic is in the time span of the weaning of a child whose arrival in the utter normality of an unknown woman's pregnancy signifies Yahweh's unfailing loyalty to His people. It is precisely in the age-long token human birth supplies of that divine fidelity that the 'sign' belongs. For 'He is with us – for us' in the assurance that recurrence of our entrustedness with offspring inherently affords.

In a setting of national crisis, a new and untried king is bewildered about his policy towards a looming threat from a potential alliance of hostility. The prophet answers the royal reluctance to 'seek a sign', i.e. to weigh the situation in the light of divine wisdom. Whether out of indecision or umbrage at the prophet's intervention at his court, Ahaz the king, declines the suggestion. Whereupon Isaiah bids him trust that, between a babe's birth and that same babe's weaning at the mother's breast – in that brief interlude – the hostile strategy he so fears will have dissipated by its own sorry logic. Meanwhile, what could be more re-assuring in national perplexity than the mystery of human parenthood, risked, fulfilled and implemented? It is the very ordinariness, not to say the anonymity, of this *almah*, this young mother of 'Immanuel'.

The Hebrew word means, simply, a 'maid', a woman of marriageable age, a girl conceiving a child and becoming thus a mother and thence a nursing woman, as ever in the timeless human scene. *Almah* has no necessary sense akin to the Greek *parthenos*, nor that 'Immanuel' is her first, her only, or somehow her 'fatherless', child. Ahaz is not being offered a miracle at which to direct investigative wonder: he is invited to ponder the assurance childbirth itself can bring and to await, through the time-span of a child's weaning, the resolution of his political fears. Meanwhile, his right posture is so to trust that he may emerge trustworthy. Hebrew prophets were adept at indicating lengths of time by vivid measure and clinching their case by lively appeal to their hearers' imagination.

What then of Isaiah 7:14 when we return to Mary and her Magnificat, to Mary whose 'Immanuel' was not a nameless infant relevant only for the length of his weaning, nor held to signify for a brief political crisis. Then there is the haunting problem, latent in all the other cases we have cited, as to how a text could arguably span so many centuries between its first apparent meaning and its allegedly destined bearing in the hidden future. Why should a virgin nativity for Jesus have been drawn from Isaiah 7 so incongruously? Was it simply that the accident of translation between *almah* and *parthenos* misled? Hardly – for even if a congruity between the two terms could be drawn from the Hebrew word, it clearly had no place in what was to signify for the Judean king.

It is equally clear that 'virgin birth' at the nativity of Jesus also had no place in what was eventually – and eventfully – signified by his life and ministry. It evidently had no mention in the 'annunciation' these had by the evangelists as Mark firmly shows. Even in Luke and Matthew the infancy introductions are plainly detached from their sequence at chapter 3 in each case.

There is no suggestion that when 'Jesus came preaching' folk were adjured to listen because choirs of angels had sung at his birth or that 'kings from the east' had worshipped at his cradle. It was only from their subsequent faith-perspective that those two Gospels were ready to supply their preface. No evangelist cited virginal origin as appeal to audience or as a clue to identity. Nor does it appear from the portrayal of Mary in the Gospels – a theme to which we must return – that her virginal significance belonged at all with the course of Jesus' ministry. There is, in that story, no light on how she may have related what ensued to her role in its birth initiation. A poem on her annunciation might muse on how she may have pondered its historic implications and have her saying:

My mother-love could well suffice
The time of infant need,

But what of manhood's hidden risk?
This call I cannot heed.

The girl who would be dedicate
To Messianic birth
Could forfeit in Gethsemane
The son she gives the earth.

His task will leave her home bereft,
His mission haunt her mind,
At length beside a felon's grave
Her broken self to find.

But such foresight, with all its poetic force, would have required an aware-ness of which, *in situ*, the Gospels show no trace. If that be so, it leaves us with the problem of that 'Song of greeting to vocation' which Luke places on her lips.

Could it be that the Song is anticipatory of what would only be appre-hended in the full event of a Christian Jesus, yet fittingly enworded for the point and personhood where all began? If so, then Mary's destiny matured only painfully and tragically into comprehension *ex eventu Christi* – a conjecture of which there are signs in the Gospels, to which we must duly come.

Meanwhile the absence of any invocation of the virginal nativity in the active ministry of Jesus as the Gospels tell it, is seconded by its complete absence also in the apostolic preaching. According to Luke in writing of their 'Acts', their preaching was centred on the Passion and the Resurrection. It is 'this Jesus whom God raised up' who is proclaimed 'in deed and word', with no plea drawn from the manner of his mothering. Paul's sole reference in Galatians 4:4 is simply to Jesus as 'born of a woman, born under the law', the first clause being a stress on common humanity, the second – only debatably – a reference to legitimate or, perhaps, levirate paternity. It would be difficult to read the classic faith about Mary into Paul's words.

The problem of his silence about the nativity of Jesus is not to be resolved by appeal to 2 Corinthians 5:16 where – in a much misread passage – he speaks of 'not knowing Christ after the flesh'. For the allu-sion is neither to Bethlehem nor to Galilee – though Paul in Jerusalem may well have had some indirect awareness of Jesus or his repute. It is to this-worldly concepts of 'the Christ', to zealot, Qumrani, or other, notions of 'Messiah', all of which, he says, are disqualified in how Jesus, Christicly, had proved to be, 'making all things new'.

We have reasonably had sundry sightings – in imagination – of the wise men coming to stand beneath the Cross to know the sequel to their natal quest, but they are not part of sacred story. We do not pause to wonder whether any of the bereaved mothers of 'the innocents' survived to contemplate the Gospel about the Cross on which their babes' contemporary became himself the victim. Shepherds of Bethlehem presumably grew old to learn of crucifixions but their recollections had no known linkage to the ultimate story of their noels to be invoked in awed corroboration.

How then are we to understand the clear credal doctrine of a virginal nativity? It is too crucial to be left to turn on a mistaken reading of a single noun between two languages. Nor can it be rightly assessed in the terms we have seen poetically drawn from retrospective reverence detecting cryptic allusions latent in hallowed texts, where readings bring themselves to what they find. Virginal nativity could not be a wistful or wilful finding of their order.

Must it not be understood as deliberate and doctrinal, a formula for a conviction only so confessed sufficiently? Let us defer the immediate question of history and actuality in order first to appreciate the impulses at work.

All has to be set in the context of time's sacrament, and of faith concerning 'the Christian Jesus'. As with earlier and lesser themes about crib and star and shepherds and Magi and a mandatory Bethlehem, so here in far deeper way, we are handling the theme of an 'advent', a 'visitation', an allegedly eternal involvement with time, with place and earthly incidence. As such the temporal dimension requires that it be dated, located, undergone, such being the requisites of history where it purports to happen. Yet – paradox though it be – no such eternal 'happening' can be seen as innovative except from the angle of a timed initiation by which alone time is aware of it. That apart, it belongs eternally with God if it ever be from Him.

Thus the existent Jesus must be one with the pre-existent Christ whom already we have encountered in preceding chapters and must again wonder at in post-existent reality in the meaning of Easter, seeing that what is not innovative is also not rescinded. Could it be that Christian theology, out of these urgencies of inner consistency about the reality of Christhood, ordained for itself the otherwise defective reading of *almah* as 'virgin' in Isaiah 7:14? Not that the criterion of a single passage could enclose the whole theme, there being – as we must see – other constraints as well, but that all would be sufficiently contained within the inclusive conviction concerning 'God in Christ'. Virginal nativity would be the safeguard, whether as symbol or as fact, of that larger truth where alone its meaning could belong and where its warrant would always be sought. The virgin Mother would be the counterpart of the Christ of God, the ultimate significance of 'handmaid to the Lord'.

[53]

But can this mean that dogma is at liberty to construct itself out of conviction almost as it will? Hardly – yet arguably on the condition of alert and steadily critical scrutiny on its own part, such as Anglican tradition requires. For, as William James observed, 'truths cannot become true till our faith has made them so'. This is the case even in the most observational realms. There is always a 'will' in the issues, whether of belief or unbelief.

Faith around Mary's motherhood of Jesus and divine Incarnation has to hold – and be held inside – conviction of the larger confidence which turns more widely still, as Chapters Five and Six must study, on vast perspectives of human history, the dynamism of human wrong and the crisis of the good. She as 'the handmaid' will always be the wondrous part in the greater whole.

Perhaps we might borrow to state it that phrase in Hebrews 8:2: 'the tent which the Lord pitched and not man'. For 'tent-pitching' was the loved imagery of John's Prologue, the *eskenosen* (1:14) of how he 'dwelt' in human midst. Or, if we take possible reading, via the Aramaic (as some have argued) the same passage, usually understood as describing 'believers', is read in the singular as relating to 'the Word made flesh' – '*who* was born, not of heredity, nor by human intercourse sought and found, but of God'. If that disputed reading holds, the verse would be the clearest formula in the Gospels concerning Mary's child.

Or faith might fall back on those strange possessives in Luke 2:49 and 1 Corinthians 3:23 – 'In my Father's . . .' '. . . Christ is God's'. What do we add, if add we must? 'Business', 'place', 'house', 'affairs' have all been suggested in the Lukan case. As for Paul's, 'Son' would be the doctrinal word to go with the genitive or, more probingly, we might say 'policy', 'answer', 'wisdom', or 'programmatic'. Or, in either case, why not 'where God belongs'?

Or again, there is that early credal summary in 1 Timothy 3:16 at a rather later point in New Testament mind-shaping. 'Without controversy' (what irony is there!) 'great is the mystery of our religion, God was manifest in the flesh . . .' 'Without naye' is Tyndale's phrase for that Greek *homologoumenos*, 'confessedly by one and all', a *nemine contradicente* of faith, concerning divine 'epiphany', as if alluding to William James' principle about how truth and faith relate.

A doctrinal formula, however, on behalf of meaning served needs its proper provisos. It is not free to be idly inventive or to exceed its Christly mandate. When this due modesty or reticence of faith are violated great illusion and error are risked. Darkly this has happened in respect of Mary. The faith in virginal nativity is no prescript for superstition, no license for fantasy.

There are three things in which its inner consistency is violated and which its doctrinal intention may not include. The first would be the use of it as mere – and arbitrary – invocation of miracle as the necessary warrant of faith. That way superstition lies. Appeal to extraneous miracle is no proper sanction for intelligent faith. Sober belief is the truer, the more honest, for its absence, seeing that integrity belongs only with soul and mind in single love.

It must follow, secondly, that exaltation of some 'Queen of Heaven' dispensing largesse has no ground in Bethlehem, still less from Christ's Gethsemane. It offends against Mary's own Magnificat. When passing into popular piety it quite misreads the meaning of her own annunciation. The *Chaire kecharitomene, Ave gratia plena* of Luke 1:28 is not, in context, about a beneficence to bestow. It is about a dignity bestowed. It is a salutation concerning her role in motherhood – 'How wonderful for you, Mary!' 'What great calling is yours.' If 'congratulation' could keep its original, and shed its trivial sense, that would be the word to tell the salutation.

It may be claimed that the principle 'Thinking it to be as *plena gratia* has come to be' is no less a case of 'faith merely a self affirming' thing but it could only be so in contravening the central, and governing, principle of the Incarnation itself, namely that 'God was in Christ reconciling the world'. Thus, in a sad subtraction, it would disown the reality from which alone it could derive its claim. When to the appeal to Mary is added the concept of her 'immaculate conception', the distortion deepens. If the thought is somehow to elude the human factor as contagious, logic would require endless 'immaculate ancestries'. We recall that Gospel genealogies are still interested in that of Joseph. Devotion to Mary is wisest to stay close to the temper of her own Song.

Thirdly, and consequently to the foregoing, the consistency of doctrinal intention leaves no room for depreciation of normal human sexuality. To be sure it *may* seem otherwise and one has to defy centuries of counter-assumption to hold it so. As William Temple noted when, prior to ordination, he pondered this item of faith, the Creeds, as he said, 'fasten attention on the wrong point' if the emphasis is on the 'unwanted human' rather than on the 'human in its wanted role'. As itself the supremely sacramental thing the Incarnation inclusively hallows the vocation into holiness of all human experience, the sexual most signally of all, ground as it ever remains of all else in culture and society.

'Mary and Magnificat' must pass to more factual questions insofar as they may be reached. Virginal nativity must share with Jesus' Resurrection as something to which there was no witness, no eye-observer. Both, in their alleged actuality, could be assessed only in their sequel, never in their incidence. For Mary the coming into pregnancy could never be accessible either to proof or to disproof. Aside from all believing reverence, in the very nature of the case it could only be an intimate and private secret. The Infancy Gospels are clear that scruple, puzzle, wonder had deep place in the story. Birth is always a societal concern, the more so when its privacies seem strange.

When, as we have seen at the outset in this chapter, faith found its conviction as to Mary's child, it might be argued that the detail could be left to silence while the divine attribution stayed. Idle curiosity had no place in letting faith tell itself. However, it is clear that in the setting of the apostolic Church, and beyond, calumny was in the air. Perhaps for outsiders, still more for adversaries, it could not be otherwise. The Gospels are ready to refer to Joseph as Jesus' 'father', and though there are 'questions' there is no losing sight of his mother in the story.

Popular curiosity, groping surmise, may well have persisted, but only vaguely in that her standing had no place in the preaching. In some quarters, though it is hard to say when, these passed into disdain and obloquy. There is the clear hint in John 8:41 when some said pointedly around the issue of 'seed': 'We were not born of fornication' and 9:34: 'Thou wast altogether born in sin and do you teach us?' Jesus, they mused, was the illegitimate child of some prostitute. It may be that the doctrine of the virgin birth was responding to such denigration.

There were other charges too, among them the claim that Jesus' father was, in fact, a Roman captain named Panthera (Pantherus) who had seduced Mary or used her in a brothel. More sinister still is the interpretation of virginal nativity as a deliberate 'cover-up' of the truth that Mary was in fact a *qadesha*, or temple 'priestess' who gave birth to Jesus in the pagan context of cultic sexuality around the *ba'alim* in sacred fertility ritual playing on the dual theme of 'husbandry'.

This view pre-supposes that such cultic practices were common in first century Galilee and readily co-existed with the rigorous monotheism of the Jerusalem Temple. It draws attention to the apocryphal Gospels and their presentation of Mary as 'dedicated' to or in a temple, as from a tiny child. Was the much older Joseph then, ever known as a 'carpenter' or 'mason', also a temple acolyte or 'guardian'?

In line with this scenario, it is sometimes argued that a 'distance' it discerns between Jesus and his mother in the Gospels of the New Testament plays into its hands. Was there, in truth, such latent antipathy between them? His frequent point about responsive faith-relation making each and all to him as 'mother, sister, brother' (Matthew 12:49–50) means, in its wide range, no exclusive disinterest in the first. Nor is the much cited 'discourtesy' of the address to her in John 2:4 a right reading of that *gunia* word, used as it is respectfully in the Greek writers, rather as one might say to the other sex: 'Man, cheer up . . .'

As we have to study in Chapter Four, the theme in Jesus' ministry is squarely that of wrestling with Messianic meaning. In this his relation with Mary plays a minimal role. Whatever we should understand about his inner consciousness in this vocation, the role of his mother in his birth-initiation was neither public nor actively a factor in its conscious pursuit. She seems at times to be uncomprehending or sharing in despair about his sanity, despite the intimacy of the Galilean circle from which he drew his family of disciples. The whole Gospel perspective has to be gathered into the meaning of 'Sonship', and then only a maternal relation in being in and for a divine mission.

So to realise brings the course of thought round again to Mary's Magnificat, sufficient as it is in its context of motherhood where mother-hood most obtains – in womb, at breast, at knee, in tears and joy. There seems to be no abstract noun from 'handmaiden' but it is the one we need. The Song draws us away from discursive things, thus far engaging us, and lifts theology into its ultimate realm of adoration and wonder.

In his early youth the 20th century French dramatist and man of letters, Paul Claudel, attended in deep unhappiness on Christmas Day, 1896, the Christmas Mass at Notre Dame de Paris. Already a precocious writer, he thought to find 'material for a few symbolist compositions'. Disgruntled, and having nothing better to do later, he returned for Vespers. Somehow he had not known of the Magnificat before. Vividly recalling his exact position 'near the second pillar at the entrance to the choir', his memoir says:

> It was at that moment that I experienced an event that has dominated my whole life. In a twinkling of an eye my heart was touched and I believed . . . with a certainty that left no place for doubt . . . All the hazards of a tumul-tuous life were unable to shake my faith . . . the eternal infancy of God, an unspeakable revelation!

That 'exultation of my whole being', as he called it, has been endlessly counter-parted throughout the long Christian tradition.

Faith's final duty to the Song of Mary is to ask about its provenance. Do we owe it simply to the literary genius of Luke? How do we take the cryptic words during her visit to her cousin: 'and Mary said . . . '? Could he conceivably have had it from her later recollection? Was he emulating the tradition of Hannah around the birth of Samuel – a tradition often renewed in retrospect to such pregnancies of promise? Or could it be that the precedent stems from the mothers of the warrior Maccabees who had better reason than Mary to sing of 'the mighty' dethroned? If so, the paradox of that echo in the days of the great Herod would only be wondrous comment on the inclusive paradox of Incarnation itself.

How Mary and Luke inter-related over her Magnificat – whether simply by kindred genius of mind or by note-comparing while they both survived – matters little factually while we have the spiritual measure in the heart of either. In Mary's case, it will perhaps be wisest to let it derive from an instinctive Hebrew piety that already cherished the fine old lyric of an exemplary Hannah and link it with Messianic musings such as might well belong with devout girlhood in Nazareth.

Yet its being, if we are right, of that order makes it all the more the abiding doxology of motherhood. In the interval – as Matthew has it – between betrothal to Joseph and bridal moving to the destined home, what womanly thoughts would not be turning, in all normality, to the prospect of a child to come? Awaiting ahead lay that perennial mystery of enwombing and of being enwombed, the amazing affinity, within the very body, of identity as a house and of a housed identity, the one achieving in the achievement of the other, and all a timed significance making its gradual and its mutual way into newness of life. Perpetual Magnificat surely belongs with that experience, given the holiness of heart that could anticipate in those ennobled and ennobling terms.

Is it not thus that what Mary sang has the reach of truth to consecrate all maternity (to choose the harder Latin term)? If so, is it not a capacity yielded by the once for all Incarnation as told on the lips of the singular Mary? For whatever be the story of conceivings, all bearing into birth is a singular experience. Hence, surely, the point of all those personal pronouns in the Song – 'My soul . . . my Saviour . . . his handmaiden . . . me blessed . . . me great things . . . our fathers.' All these, not least the last, would be apt on all mothers' tongues, with that awed sense of being in the long and honoured role of 'all generations'. Any Messianic thoughts apart, all mothers in their utter indispensability have shared the making of the generations, the 'great chain of being', the procreating which 'keeps the eternal creation alive' via 'the tender mercy of our (human) God'.

'Messianic thoughts apart' – how should we surmise of them in respect of Mary and the annunciation? For they were made explicit in the terms it told – '. . . His mercy as He spake . . .' In answer, Christian faith – at its clearest – has always understood that the Incarnation is as much a truth about ourselves and our human vocation as it is about God and His 'magnanimity' towards us humans. There is no accident in the Latin play on words. It was and is the strange prerogative of divine greatness to need and seek our recruited part and being thus recruited is the high dignity of 'our low estate', the royal road to our serving benediction.

Perhaps nowhere was this meaning better caught than once in a sermon of Bernard of Clairvaux where, as if anticipating W. H. Auden's words about 'your power of choosing to conceive the child who chooses you', Bernard said:

> Answer the angel speedily. Speak the word and receive the word. Offer what is yours and conceive what is of God. Give what is temporal and embrace what is eternal . . . Let your humility put on boldness and your modesty be clothed with trust . . . In this one thing, O Virgin, fear not presumption: open your heart to faith.

How finely he had caught both the anguish and the ecstacy and so known in his own male soul the 'sign of Mary', this muting of aspiration in surrender, this inner lowliness in the very register of honour. Such is ever the way of incarnating mission, of what a musical borrowing for theology might call 'the instrumentation of the script'. It is we who have to say:

> Annunciation, have your way.
> My soul and body yield.
> Some strange divine complicity
> My readiness has sealed.

'The human form', as Wordsworth thought is ever 'an index of delight' but never more so than when yielded into hallowing.

But what should we say of the apparent subversion, in Magnificat, of the powers that be in the world? Why did the Song, like Simeon in his Nunc Dimittis, use, according to Luke, that past tense: 'He has put down the potentates from their thrones and lifted up the *tapeinous*, the oppressed' who languished under them? How, in a mere babe in arms (never under arms) could the old man have 'seen salvation'? Hannah's Song had used more hortatory language: 'Talk no more so grossly proudly', while Mary, like many things Biblical, is proleptic, anticipating here and now what can only be awaited in time ahead. That, in several psalms, could well be the first sense of being 'begotten', as in Psalm 2:7: 'This day have I begotten thee', as meaning: 'I have put thee into the position of a son as though I had actually begotten thee,' pledging commission and protection.

It has been thought noteworthy that Mary's song refers to 'oppressors and oppressed' as persons, not to 'power' or 'poverty' in the abstract – a point which has weighed with contemporary liberationists in theology who require that we should read the text in the concrete, since the words are performative and not idly descriptive. 'Let my people go' is a demand and not a wistful yearning – unless the latter promised action.

Doubtless this sort of exegesis drew Karl Marx and Friedrich Engels to recruit the Magnificat for their famous Communist Manifesto. Familiar, if not to them, was the story of the 11th century King Robert of Sicily, who, dozing briefly during Evensong, awoke with a start to hear voices chanting: 'He has put down the mighty from their thrones,' and seized his sword to strike against subversive priests.

But how does such martial reading tally with what Mary surely meant in reference to herself, or to the coming accent of Jesus' own Beatitudes? Some have thought that Simeon and Anna, for their part, *were* anticipating a political Messiah whereas Mary – or Luke – *can* be read as reversing this to indicate one whose preaching would overturn them by the principle of 'enemies to be loved'. That would be in line with Kosuke Koyama's *No Handle on the Cross*. When visiting the Kremlin from Japan, he queued to view the corpse of Lenin and noted how the hands were clenched as fists, in telling contrast with the wounded hands of Christ.

Yet, while there is no trace of 'holy war' in the Magnificat, it is feasible to read its 'low estate' theme as conjoining both a physical plight or burden *and* a deliberate set of mind and will. If so, it would take us to something like Matthew 11:28–30, linked with the Beatitudes, where we have always to enquire: 'Who and why were these heavy-laden?' One answer has said 'the heavy burden' of meticulous observing of the endless details of Torah as interpreted by the Rabbis – the burden that has made many orthodox keepers eager for the *eruv*, a 'free zone' of exemption. But Jesus' 'learn of me' has echoes of the call of wisdom, the 'come unto me, ye unlearned' of Ecclesiasticus (51:23–27), where 'wisdom', however exacting its tuition, would spell 'rest'.

In that event, with 'disciple' as 'learner', discipleship to the Son Mary awaited would be a calling into the strenuous reaches of social justice such gentle wisdom sought. 'The learning of the lowly', of that order, would be the Christ's way of dethroning the brutal powers that followed only the principles of power, of fear, of force and subjugation – the 'yoke' of the heavy-handed.

It would be naïve to consider Mary with Magnificat consciously thinking these thoughts. Her seeing the future as a happened past was a devout, Hebraic way of anticipating the fulfilment somehow latent in the immediate and highly charged meaning of her experience, as Luke's narrative purports to tell it. Meanwhile the call to destiny certainly itself fulfilled the principle it had invoked. For Magnificat was the voice of 'the lowly and meek' aware within of 'great things'.

From where, too, did she draw that phrase about 'the imagination of their hearts', in respect of the politics of the proud? It seems to have been Tyndale's coining for the Greek *dianoia* for which 'scattering' is an apt word. For 'thoughts' of rank, of office, of rule, crowd in upon the covetous and the power-wielding, in conspiracies of cunning, the corrupting counsels of power-perpetuation and the deviousness of politics.

Yet, in the paradox alike of the Incarnation and the Song, is there no place for the hallowing of power as indispensable to the due 'filling of the hungry', the due honouring of the otherwise oppressed? Is not the Lord too 'showing strength with His arm'? Would tyrants be otherwise 'put to flight'? What of that other, more ultimate doxology about 'King of kings, and Lord of lords', made so triumphant in the music of Handel? Revelation 19:16, it has been argued, underwrites for civil order and the political realm a right to exist and operate, if not free of ecclesiastical obligation, at least its ready tool. The 'lords' and 'kings' who are possessed in the clauses by the divinely supreme One have, therefore, a genuine suzerainty of their own. The words could be read that way, though papal and other ecclesiology would subordinate it. The 'divine right of kings', at which the verses hint, can only be had as 'right' if also had as 'subject' to God, since the 'divine' word governs either way.

That issue, though implicit in Mary's Song, is worlds away from the vocation she celebrates. All its implications have to be drawn on and into the ministry of the son she bore.

Meanwhile Magnificat holds one final meaning, a meaning for us all. When Paul writes in Galatians 4:19 to the well-loved folk there and tells them: 'I travail again in birth till Christ be formed in you,' it is doubtful that he had Mary in mind. For, as we saw, he made no use – unless here – of the virginal nativity of Jesus in his ministry. Yet the analogy between the womb of mothering and the soul-forming of his ministry is apt to his mind. It is confirmed by the one noun *morphe* he uses of the Incarnation in Philippians 2:5–11 and the verb in Galatians. In this sense 'bearers of Christ' is vocation for all. The service to 'the Word made flesh', which Christian faith sees to have been supremely Mary's own, invites all who love and heed her Song into a like readiness to say: 'Let it be with me according to Thy word.' Magnificat becomes a personal surrender, a defining perception of the selves we are.

If this is where devotion and theology alike come home in Mary's Song, they need one abiding caution, one discipline for the soul of the one and the mind of the other. It is that the formula, or the invocation 'Mary, Mother of God' is darkly and (if we have Muslims in mind) dangerously ambiguous if said without the words '. . . the Son'. It is vital and urgent for any theology always to avoid saying what it cannot truly mean in the act of saying what it seeks to mean. Otherwise, the truth it tells becomes at the same point untruth – a hazard which has been disastrously the case down long centuries.

The Incarnation itself is disowned and abnegated if – even unwittingly

– we have implied that God in His eternity – ever underived – was in debt to human fashioning, He only and for ever divinely One. We must keep faith alert for what we have earlier called 'Time's sacrament'. Eternally Self-sufficing, it is precisely out of such 'sufficing' *vis-à-vis* our human condition that His 'being-who-He-is' has this 'becoming-on-our-behalf', time-told, yet in the telling for ever what never 'came to be' other than the One who eternally was and is, 'God blessed for evermore'. Mary could only ever be 'Mother of God' for never, ever, being such.

What is at issue here both for faith and piety takes us into divine Sonship and the chapter that follows.

CHAPTER FOUR

Our Lord Jesus Christ

It would seem odd to think or write of the 'christening' of Jesus. For 'to christen' is defined as 'giving a name at baptism' – a rite performed by others with (*qua* adult) or without (*qua* infant) the consent of the vital party involved. The baptism of Jesus in the Gospels that tell of it was not of that order. Yet there was a 'naming' of him in his earliest days, as reportedly indicated at his conception, and that 'Jesus name' with its meaning of 'here God saves' was exactly what Christian faith received and told as his whole significance. In that way the historic faith was only taking up and ensuring as identity into the centuries the reality he was seen to embody in his entire story. It would then be right and sound to see him as 'christened' in and by the Christianity to which his being who and how he was gave historic rise and perpetuity. Christian faith was its verdict on the meaning of his Hebrew name and a historic 'naming' of him in its terms.

That sense of the matter is well captured in the fourfold descriptive that made its early appearance in the first of New Testament Scriptures – 1 Thessalonians 1:3 – namely, 'Our Lord Jesus Christ'. In the phrase lay the origin of the later Creed. It told of a personhood – Jesus, fulfilled in a drama of vocation – the Christ, set in the high esteem of discipleship – Lord, and incorporating in all these capacities a living community using the personal plural pronoun 'our'. Such within a quarter century of his narrative was his 'recognition', his 'reputation', in effect his 'christening' in that the perceived meaning of his personal name had been collectively realised as 'the Christ of God'.

That is to describe and define the historic proceeding Jesus underwent – which some (as we must defer to Chapter Six) would demand to disallow. That it happened this way, that there did come about a historic faith *in* him in these terms, there is no question. But it would be bizarre to think somehow of disciples and apostles as his 'godparents'. 'Christen' is an active verb, a performative event undertaken in the will and not merely undergone. The whole conviction in 'the Christian Jesus' and these chapters is that the Christhood the Church found in Jesus was verily the Christhood of his achieving and of his intent.

What we always have to ask about history is whether there is coherence between event and narration, between what indeed happened and how what happened meant. Historians worth their name are always verdict seekers and, by the same token, risk-takers. What faith, too, has to ask about Jesus and the resulting New Testament – for result from him it was – is what the event must have been to come into this documentation. There was a Jesus, story-ing and to be storied, who was storied as the 'our Lord Jesus Christ' of whom faith tells. What came to be confessed concerning him derived from whom he arrived to be in the immediacies of time and place. To acknowledge 'incarnation' would then be to read God and a history aright and to have the identity by which this Jesus had been – would for ever remain – the Christ. So much for the performative 'christening', whereby faith told him.

The actual 'naming' of this Jesus, at the earliest moment of Jewish fidelity to covenant, followed devoutly from all we have just studied of Mary and Magnificat. The ultimate adulthood would make good its Hebrew meaning in ways not first foreseen. The baptism of Jesus takes us with the evangelists to the River Jordan. With its immediate sequel in 'temptations' in the desert, it was an inauguration that casts its meaning over all that ensued.

It is clear from three successive 'If . . .'s that what faith later understood as 'incarnational' had to do with supremely practical things, with 'policies' we might almost say, and in no way with 'ontology', or 'status' other than actional and needing to be wrought in deeds. We do not come into 'the Word made flesh', like Philip Larkin in his 'Church Going' – 'only when I'm sure there's nothing going on'. 'The artifice of eternity' is not that way. Everything is situational. Jesus' 'Sonship' is vocation, with discernment and intent.

The issue of Messiahship is everywhere, in fully Hebraic order, though it has often been argued that Christology has Graeco-Latin, even pagan, origins as divine ranking requisite to Emperors. On the contrary, Hebrew faith was full of 'divine agencies' whereby Yahweh's purposes towards His people were effectuated, as supremely in the ministry of prophethood. The 'servant' word in this context was almost synonymous with the 'son' word and, as in the case of Jeremiah (1:5), could even be with birth and a mother's womb. For

> Great every mother with child, in her son,
> Her body's deep mystery tenderly waking
> life in the making.

'Servant' and 'son' were frequently applied to the sundry and elusive concepts of God's 'Messiah', just as earlier they had been understood to denote the 'chosen people' themselves, as when the psalmist (105:15) warns potential enemies where they are in transit: 'Touch not mine anointed and do my prophets no harm.'

Thus the 'Sonship' of Jesus that is being interrogated in the wilderness is confronted with issues of its 'servanthood', the strategy – we might almost say – of his part in the purpose of God. Aim for economic plenty: let 'divine sonship' banish material hunger. 'Turn stones into bread' and ensure a bought allegiance that need not venture into other realms where humans more essentially yearn.

Or use the psalmist's assurance in divine text – as surely any 'son/servant' might (91:11–12) – to float amazingly down from the high, high pinnacle of the Temple. Folk in the crowded court below will be yours for ever by a credulous wonder, obviating all sterner tests of Messianic will and wisdom.

Or, most cynical of all, 'seek the political kingdom: it is the one to which all other things are added.' Be realist to know that Satan never casts out Satan: your only hope is alliance with his ruses, his cunning, his deceits and necessary hates. 'Worship me and all shall be yours.'

Messiahship at the threshold will not be counselled into compromise. Significantly all three are countered and answered, not because they have no point to make, but because they violate the faith-keeping with God that must be Messiah's writ and warrant, the very substance of his 'Sonship'. So the response each time invokes what belongs with God: authority, inviolability, worship. By his Satan 'departing for a season', Luke (4:13) has us understand that the issues in the desert encounter persisted throughout the ministry, even to the taunting form of the plea: 'Come down from the Cross and we will believe.' Hence too the economy of healing signs and their non-use as inducement to discipleship.

Thus 'Jesus came preaching.' It was a message of 'God's Kingdom' already real and present by the sheer fact of being told of, yet also ever needing to be made real in, the ongoing future by dint of obedience to its claim. 'The Word made flesh' was thereby 'enfleshed' in the vivid imagery of spoken parable, in beatitude and aphorism, 'gladly heard' by common folk. It held an inherent authority, refreshingly free from the citation habit of the text-bound rabbis. There was a kindling appeal in his 'But I say to you . . .' as if inviting them to a like liberation from enslavement of mind, such as 'the kingdom' meant by its message of the immediacy of God to daily life and the dignity of every personal self.

That sense of common worth informed the very fibre of the parables. Of course, they mirrored local idiom and familiar culture where, for example, necklaces were more likely to be of coins than of pearls and vine-yards worked for absent landlords, but they told of human experience all could recognise as theirs. One did not have to ask about the ethnic iden-tity of a wayward lad in his 'far country', nor locate the field of 'tares' exclusively in Galilee, nor confine unemployment in the market-place to Neapolis or Tiberias.

This human inclusiveness of the parables reflected the perception Jesus had of 'your heavenly Father', the finite carefulness he took to be the nature of the Infinite. 'Abba, Father' was his constant prayer, and his assurance to his listeners: 'One there is who . . .' and then a variety of themes having to do with solicitude, forgiveness, provision and concern. The very 'communicability' of divine Lordship in these terms to all and sundry 'who had ears to hear' was the expressed meaning of his own Sonship. Only from within could it be so affirming to the world around.

For the inter-defining between Jesus and the New Testament docu-ment which we are tracing in this chapter, it is clear that his verbal teaching was the decisive factor. Most New Testament scholarship is agreed that crucial to the Gospels' formation was a collection of Jesus' sayings, a gathered source often called 'Q', believed to underlie the three Gospels called 'synoptic'. It is fair to say that a teaching Jesus was thus the founding dimension of *any* written preservation of his presence in history. A basic element in 'the Word made flesh' lay in 'words left mem-orable' – a preaching fit to undergird what became a faith in Incarnation.

Furthermore, Matthew plainly collects those sayings – belonging as they did to an itinerant – in a 'mount-based Sermon', where he assembles 'his disciples', in allusion to the tribes of Israel receiving from Moses their defining Torah. Matthew's Gospel establishes the teaching Jesus as thus inaugurating a new 'people of God' via the wisdom of his new Moses. He is gathering what was also scattered by many roadsides, heard in many byways. He is narrating journeys where incidents were steadily rein-forcing the dicta he has purposely unified in the single sermon form, leaving the parables, for the most part, to the itinerary. It is the incidents which corroborate the things taught, as when 'a woman of Canaan' is schooled to have from Jewishness what no 'Gentile' can receive except by Jewish grace, namely a surmounting of the differential (15:21–28): Or when Luke records how patience behaves in the face of racial enmity by moving gently 'to another village' (9:51–56).

Throughout, in this all too brief saga of walking and talking in what Muslims might call 'the path of God', there are two areas of reference to which Jesus' teaching is responsive and which serve to make it episodic as might scenery in a drama and text deploy its context. The one is the slow

education of the disciples, the other is the growing unease around establishment's controversy.

The disciples, with their zeal and loyalty, their confusion and ambition,
were a steady foil to their Lord. Indeed, his will for them, patience with
them and purpose through them, were central features of his ministry.
Faith, as the Church later reached it, in the Incarnation itself could then
recognise in discipled recruitment within it the vital clue to the reality of
the Church itself as ministering with Christ. Hence again the role of 'apostolic saints' in Christian liturgical tradition and hence again the naming
of two Gospels – whatever their un-named authorship – after immediate
disciples with two others of later calling. Hence again their vital role in
the literary tradition of their traced companionship with Jesus and Paul's
urgent claim not to be exempt since his Damascus vision had qualified
him differently as a 'Jesus familiar'.

There was a long rabbinic tradition of 'learners' attendant on their
teachers and perusing and debating round a text as the given oracle of
hallowed lore. Or votaries, as in Qumrân, were enclosed in the rigorous
confines of ascetic order, isolating legitimacy in separatist fervour. The
tuition of Peter, James and John, their colleagues and associates, belong
squarely with the open road and a situational school. The Gospels became
this way the sort of texts they are, which is another evidence of the intimate inter-shaping of narrative in flow and narrative on page. The story
was perpetuated as wanted for what it had comprised in human knowing.

Parables were taken further in because these 'pupils' enquired. 'Signs'
were interpreted because they were first ill-read. Naïveties were checked
and righted by reflection on the weight and mystery of human ills or the
travail present in their redemption. There was a cumulative tutorial in the
very disillusioning of their optimism, the toughening of their realism after
their own separate ventures. When at length Jesus ordained the bread and
wine in his 'remembrance', it was not that all these other recollections
could ever fade from mind: it was that they might be set and framed in
the most significant lesson of all.

The crucial theme of this companioning education, as the Gospels see
it, was the Messianic meaning. In some sense this had been the impulse of
their recruitment and, expectantly, of their response. But it was fraught
with deep and hazardous ambiguity. Hence, it would seem, the enigmatic
quality of reference to it and of what is variously dubbed 'the Messianic
secret'. Open use of the term would have been calamitous, inasmuch as
the 'who?' of Messianic identity could only be resolved in the 'how' of
Messianic policy.

It is within the meaning of the Incarnation itself that Jesus wrestled
steadily with the issue in the light of the logic discernibly developing in

the course of his ministry and its reception in the world. A crucial point of crisis came in the withdrawal from activity to the remote Banias region, at Caesarea Philippi, in the foot-hills of Hermon. 'Whom do people say I am?' (Matthew 16:13–23, Mark 8:27–29 and Luke 9:18–20) was about the impact of his mission on the populace in respect of its most ultimate burden. 'Whom do you say that I am?' extended that sifting, both of them and their reactions, to their intimate affections and fears.

Their verdict in its anxious confidence only heightened for Jesus the inner definition in the crisis of sonship and obedience, seeing that the case Peter thought himself confessing was so far from what *ex eventu* the Church would know as 'the mind of Christ'. Meanwhile the path for the disciples would pass into utmost dereliction until 'Whom do you say that I am?' could have veritable telling. For both his and their Gethsemane, in its contrasted undergoing, lay awaiting them ahead.

The Messianic 'question' was implicit in the second area of significance in a reading of the Jesus scene, namely issues with hierarchy both legal and social. To see the disciples educated situationally is to realise how many of the situations concerned the scribal and the priestly in the prestige of office. Sundry items of his teaching, around the character of Yahweh, the writ of the Sabbath, the authority of texts, the place of conscience, set them at odds with him and he with them. Readers of the Gospels can trace a sort of cumulative crisis deepening from 'murmurings and contentions' into the final pattern of the Cross. Jesus was reproached frequently before he was rejected finally. 'The cup for his drinking', of which he often spoke, was shaped in its contents by the experience he underwent. That – as one writer has it – 'he willed to be remembered among his friends' as 'one who had a cup in his hand' in what would become the Eucharist, was an image maturing through his story and only so poetically right at the close.

One central theme the challenge of establishment to his Sonship contrived to focus was the role of the Temple – the very Sonship on which his ministry proceeded in the liberties that it claimed. What was latent throughout, but could only later be understood, was that he would be and become, in himself, what the Temple had so long enshrined. The clue lies in the 'place of the Name' tradition whereby – as the great Solomon had prayed at its dedication – Yahweh had pledged 'My Name shall be there' (1 Kings 8:29, 9:3 and Deuteronomy 12:11). The Temple had renewed and perpetuated that first sense of divine 'location' told in 'tentedness in the midst of the camp' during nomadic days. That 'spreading of the tent' could provide the final imagery for the Incarnation (John 1:14). When Jesus 'spake of the temple of his body' (John 2:21), the evangelist was setting that faith in the earlier context of issues between Jesus and

Jerusalem's supreme insignia. The Gospels make close association between teaching and the Temple and charge concerning it figured crucially in Jesus' trial.

But, leaving to later chapters points that wait on all the foregoing, why should this emerging *mise-en-scène* be understood, or even conjectured, by Jesus as Messianic? We are arguing here for 'a Christian Jesus', himself inwardly in the narrative, personally minded in the terms that emerging Christian faith and Scripture believed and told of him. The sceptic, whom anon we must confront, would say that this affinity is there only because the faith contrived the narrative and did so with no leave of 'the real Jesus'.

Yet a credal inventiveness casting Jesus, for faith's purposes, in a role he never played, becomes itself well-nigh incredible, seeing that communal anticipations of 'Messiah' were so far removed from the contours of that later faith, so that we are returned to Jesus as its only sufficient author. The Gospels must then be seen, not only *about* him but *from* him in the main fabric of their characterisation of his mission and himself.

Where then, from within all the qualities we have traced in the evidences of his ministry, preaching and healing in the actuality of 'the kingdom of his Father', did perception of Messianic clue eventuate – a question which reaches to the very heart of 'incarnation'?

Answer seems to lie in the tradition of prophethood, its suffering, and either in their relation to the God of their sending. On the ground it seemed clear enough that a total crisis was developing around Judaica, his and theirs, he the nuisance and they hierarchs. It could also be supposed that the prudency argument of Jewish authority would be first tempted and then constrained to hand the problem he had become to the Roman authority, thus politicising the things at stake, thus, in turn, requiring a self-defending Jesus also to politicise his meanings. That way, the third temptation, lay a treachery. Those meanings, at their deepest core, required fidelity to the past of their wording through the present of their tribulation.

Was this the set of mind that brought that language about 'the cup my Father gives', that could speak allusively to a 'baptism' to be undergone, an 'exodus' to face? (John 18:11, Luke 9:31 and 12:50). Terminating the mission, foregoing the vocation, fleeing the territory – these were no option. The situation was akin to that which great prophets had faced, in which suffering was the only form of fidelity, of the tenacity which, by not letting truth be forfeit to wrong, could avail to redeem it. For all such agencies in trust with the divine word knew, in their innermost hearts, that by the very fact of their sentness, there was a divine 'sympathy' with them in what that sending spelled for them of pain and loneliness and agony. To sense some divine indifference to these 'mission costs' would cancel any authenticity in the vocation they knew they had. If Yahweh was ever there in the sending, He was there also in the suffering.

In this way, prophethood – on both counts – foreshadowed Messiahship and, via Messiahship, New Testament Christology. God was *with*, in these prophets, what was *upon* them from their being such. By that precedent, might there not be, somewhere, a 'serving-in-travail' where the divine and the human came entirely together in a unison that was more than 'sympathy' in being utmost co-activity? If so, serving Messiahship would in truth be divine Sonship. If so again, then where God was most divinely active would correspond to a situation where the human wrongness in society was most tragically measureable in those terms.

It would seem that exactly such a double situation is the clue to the parable of the husbandmen and the messengers which occurs in three Gospels and which played a large part in the immediate context of Jesus' arrest. In the flux of historical time, no single event could be that situation comprehensively but one occasion might express it quintessentially. If so, the crucifying of Jesus could fully qualify as such – an event which Christian faith came to see in just those terms as 'the sin of the world'.

On the face of it, in the famous parable, it would seem utter folly to send 'the son', in view of the desperate handling of the servants. The truth, however, is that the occupiers had brought themselves down a spiral of ill-doing and ill-will. Their first impulsive hostility has made deepening acts of defiance congenial. The 'absence' of the owner tells how real their entrustment is but they are conspiring to contest his right itself. Possession – as the adage says – is 'nine tenths . . .'. If they can contrive to make it permanent, the vineyard is theirs. The original issue about a year's dues has been overtaken by the will to ultimate rejection. Such is the nature of human 'dominion' as never ready for the divine relation it duly has and tells, but prone ever to subvert and repudiate it.

The mission of 'the son' on the Lord's part is precisely responding to this grim evidence of how things are. Only the filial 'heir' can meet the situation in its own evil terms, for only he – unlike the servants – brings home that ultimate register of a sovereignty answering its own subversion, no less, at human hands. The tenants react in climax to their evil logic: 'This is the heir: come let us kill him and the inheritance will be ours.'

The parable has other import in relation to the old Hebraic imagery of 'people in their land' as a 'planted fruiting into righteousness', but this is the minor key in the major text of inclusive human wrong at odds with the ultimate in divine experience at the hands of human liability with crea-turehood in trust. 'They perceived that he spake of them' (Matthew 21:45) can truly be widened to describe all humans in the inclusive privilege of our custody of a good creation – of which Judaic exceptionality was always an intended sign. What was retributive in the immediate setting of the parable becomes redemptive – in the final realism it tells about us – by the son's tragedy at human hands. This is the Messianic dimension of 'come let us kill him' which Christian faith beyond the crucifixion could identify as the parable's silent clue to how the Cross should be understood as ever belonging in, or to, God.

It was uncannily in terms of the husbandmen parable that the ministry of Jesus came to its climax in the events of Holy Week. It had all the marks of a rising drama culminating, via his final challenge to the Temple, in an arrest in the Garden and the subsequent dual arraignment in the strictly Judaic idiom of 'blasphemy' and religious 'pretension', and thence into the requisite role of Roman 'law' wielding the power of the extreme sentence. The mind and will behind the Beatitudes came into a Gethsemane of 'agony', through the lying-in-wait of these human structures, ecclesial and imperial, and – in both capacities – all too human in the instincts motivating their behaviour. The one factor prevailed on the other because both had self-interests in common. Caiaphas and Pilate were indeed strange bed-fellows but the event that united them became a sort of historic exegesis of the human world in its dark capacities, religious and political. 'That it should come to this!' in a sequence out of Galilee and the tidings spread across its hills and in its village haunts about 'your heavenly Father knows and cares' was, and is, the supremely ironic commentary from which a faith could take its rise and find itself in love and hope.

Yet that, in truth, was how it happened. The whole case here – and any time – for 'the Christian Jesus' is this sustained and reciprocal relation between the 'where' of faith's origins and the 'what' of faith's finding. There are those, as a later chapter must allow, who would say that this narrative from Galilee to Gethsemane and the Cross is only the shaping of a faith, meaning by the charge that 'only believing made it so'. It is proper to turn the suspicion on its head. What made 'the believing so' if not 'the shaping of the faith' in the very forge of the events? What ensues in history is never irrelevant to what preceded it.

> . . . the words (the deeds) sufficed
> To compel the recognition they preceded . . .

So that the verdict they had honestly reached told the meaning they possessed.

To live in that confidence about Jesus of Nazareth was the experience of the apostolic Church. It was a verdict communally reached out of deep persuasives from the Hebrew past seen as divinely implemented in what transpired in Jesus to underwrite his identifying as the Christ. The later telling of that confidence loved to ground itself in being 'according to the Scriptures'.

In line with the tremendous irony noted, the witness was also reached out of utmost dissuasives in the tragic circumstances through which the disciples had survived the story of their Master crucified. When later they or their successors could write of 'that which we have seen and heard and handled' (1 John 1:1–3) the 'handling' when they reached the climax had only been either 'forsaking', 'or sleeping through' a crisis of utter despair they had no will or wit to comprehend. 'The winepress he trod' alone was for them a grim 'undiscipling' of all they had ever known, a bleakness where they could hope no longer. When Peter struggled to do so, irresolute in a distant curiosity, he was only the more completely undone.

It was from this abyss of desolation and defeat that the apostolic Church derived. It was not an abyss of treachery but the far more prostrating one of incapacity to know what loyalty must mean with this Messiah. There was burial of the crucified – as the faith would always insist as a crucial article of its confession – but the utmost measure of their dereliction was their absence from it. It turned on the impulse of a hitherto unknown follower to undertake, with high personal devotion, the obsequies of Jesus, and loyal women 'beheld where he was laid'.

We do well to come to the meaning of the Resurrection from this effective forfeiture, in bewilderment and tragedy, of the disciples' antecedent assurance about the teaching, caring, itinerating Jesus in the meaning of 'God's Kingdom'. It was a quite unwilled and unforeseen forfeiture which only a larger, fuller logic around that shared ministry could retrieve and repair. What that logic was and how it did so had to belong with all the antecedents that had physically ended in that burial, his in the sepulchre and theirs in his by the lostness of all they had lived for with him.

His 'being risen' was never witnessed as an event nor, by its nature, could it be. The only tangible evidences would be the 'emptiness' of a burial place. But that purely visual, material circumstance could never ensure the reality it might signify, since conjecture or ill-reading or hazard would always wait on its significance. Faith's 'He is not here' would be of a different order from detective case-making.

Of what order could it be? Of what order was it? We do well to go in answer to where Christian faith at length found its ripe *confessio* and let the resurrection narratives, with their themes of shared meals, of hands on wounds and awed encounters, take their place there also as the telling of a final fullness. To do so will be to hold with the point that stays in view here throughout, namely the mutual nexus between what came into faith and what belonged in event, between theology and history.

That ripe *confessio*, with its root in Messianic hope, arrived to tell of an eternal/temporal, of an advent and ascension, of a 'coming down and a going hence'. Incarnation had been the occasion where, the means whereby. It meant divine disclosure recruiting human personhood in the time and place of days 'made flesh', both out of, and again into, eternity. Faith learned to think of 'the pre-existent Christ' and thus of 'the post-existent Christ'. These did not mean some physicality there 'before all worlds' nor some ongoing physicality beyond the clouds of an 'ascension'. For to think that way would be to aver, or imply, that no 'incarnation' had ever happened. To be 'made flesh' was to occupy an interlude. For only by 'interlude' could the eternal 'enter' time, and only in time's history, somewhere, somewhen, could the will to 'enter' transpire, seeing that time's history is where we humans are, we the humans of the intended benediction in such 'visitation from on high'.

'Mission initiated, mission accomplished' would be the divine order of that 'day of the Lord'; neither – in the divine mind – was either innovative or rescinded. They derived from and they stayed with the unchanging quality of the Lord they had revealed in the immediacy of the Messiah, 'the Word', 'the flesh', they had willed for their purpose. What was divine advent was enterprised in human terms by the 'handmaid of the Lord', birth, as we have seen, being his 'first necessity'. Likewise, divine accomplishment transpired in the 'high exalting' – as Paul had it – which was resurrection/ascension, the return into the abiding meaning of a 'history' rising into the glory where it had always been and whither it would by right return, pointedly signalled by an empty grave.

The central theme of this 'mission initiated, mission achieved' was the Cross of Jesus as of 'one slain before the foundation of the world'. It gathered into one all the antecedents of the teacher becoming 'perfect through suffering' as 'the pioneer and achiever' of the faith that was to be. The Incarnation, by its own divine momentum, would be 'even to the death of the Cross'. How else, then, should that 'death with Incarnation' be 'glorified' in the terms it possessed if not by resurrection, by resurrection inseparable from 'ascension'. That sepulchre which had its 'before' in travail must have its 'after' in a 'glory had before the world was' (John 17:5). What more aptly than an empty grave could tell it so?

The Gospels, as we must explore more fully elsewhere, see that 'entering into glory' as an extended event – extended and signified for better comprehension by disciples who would be the crucial factor in its telling and its comprehending. There was – as we must conclude – a gradual but finally decisive sense of the end of physicality and the hard awakening to how that tenancy in the body had been the timely, and entirely apposite, self-giving of the eternal Lord. Such 'grasping' of the Resurrection was one with the birthing of the Church into faith. It turned on the evidences on which the Gospels rely but it belonged more ultimately still with the love and power of God most high.

Faith in the Resurrection understands a kind of frontier situation, or – one might say – a watershed, a Rubicon to which one comes as where the factual historical bank shares, as all rivers must, the thither bank, the farther side that is eternal. The transit, so to speak, is bridged – for comprehension – by a sort of inter-mediacy where 'body' belongs and does not belong, can still serve to 'certify' but must not be clutched as if still continuous with what had been known before. Its proof-carrying wounds must be discernible, ensuring that identify stays in no doubt. But it could only be poetically true to sing of 'wounds yet visible above in beauty glorified'. For their physicality is left behind at the frontier and only – what the hymn surely meant – their one-time significance eternally abides. For Incarnation indeed concludes but only in being for ever conclusive about God. It endures as the living episode of His self-giving.

That the Resurrection narratives can be rightly appreciated in these terms as tuition, both of apostles and ourselves, of those 'seeing' and those 'not seeing', about the crucified Jesus is not in doubt, if we understand that frontier aright. Hence the verifying tokens, the sequences, the re-enacting of familiars, the re-instating of 'forsakers' – all plainly comprising an interlude having a decisive close. How futile, indeed how darkly tragic, otherwise, a mere 'empty tomb' would be. 'They have taken away . . .' would, otherwise, have stayed a gnawing anguish'. 'I know not where' a long, lingering lament.

Is it not this frontier situation which is captured in 'a cloud received him out of their sight' (Acts 1:9) – 'cloud' being ever the symbol, Biblically, of what waits upon the divine presence? It would be contradicting the whole meaning of the Incarnation to imagine some kind of endless 'space journey'. Christian art sometimes visualised a hand reaching out of the cloud to welcome home the Son, just as the medieval York Passion Play had it: 'Sende downe a cloude, Fadir deare.' As W. H. Auden had it of incarnate birth, 'The flesh united to the Word without magical transformation,' so was 'flesh disunited from the Word,' not in any undoing of its meaning but by virtue of the completion of the earthly task. Eternity had enlisted from time the place for a history that only time could afford to it: time yielded back to eternity the history-maker and to the glory of his history-making which would remain unfailing in its trust and memory.

Surely then the poem of John Updike has it wrong.

Make no mistake: if He rose at all, it was as His body,
If the cells' dissolution did not reverse,

the molecules reknit, the amino acids rekindle,
the Church will fall.

He misses the Rubicon of time into eternity Christ's exaltation had to be
and misses also how nativity into time belongs ever with eternity in the
purposeful tenancy of 'body' from womb to tomb. Resurrection 'appearances' are part of that Rubicon lovingly entailing the education of
disciples as, for them, a period between the changing meanings of
'Emmanuel', the familiarly immediate and the wonderingly universal.

Only so do we have the Incarnation and the Ascension in due – not to
say credible – mutual relation, neither cancelling the meaning of the other
but holding them in one as the drama of God's love for humankind. Do
we not have it so in the language of the history-maker in Hebrews 10:5
and 7: 'When he comes into the world he says . . . "A body hast Thou
prepared me . . . Lo I come (in the volume of the book it is written of me)
to do Thy will, O God."'?

The New England poet Robert Frost sees the 'education' and gives it
cogent wording.

. . . God's own descent
Into the flesh was meant
As a demonstration
That the supreme merit
Lay in risking spirit
In substantiation.

'Risk' indeed was there in the meaning of infancy. With manhood and
ministry, it deepens into what is more than 'demonstration'. For 'demonstration' suffices only if it incorporates our distance from perceiving it. Its
'risk' lies not only in our finite frailty: it belongs in our dark perversity.
'Even the death of the Cross' is the measure of how far it needs – and it
avails – to reach. Only there, and so, could it belong commensurably with
this human world. Infancy would be the eloquent prelude when 'Unto us
a child is born', yet only in an adulthood whereby 'unto us a Son was
given'. If truly 'unto us', it must culminate in 'acquaintance with grief' and
pass into the Passion of 'a man of sorrows'.

That so in truth it did proved that the 'demonstration' came surely to
pass. For from it a faith was born, a faith that would learn to tell how it
had been as something 'seen and heard and handled'. The Incarnation
would be verifiable and verified in 'the body of Christ', the peoplehood
that itself came into being by the experience of becoming verifiers. So
much is the force of that personal pronoun 'Our', owning its first credal
words that could be said in any order: 'Christ – Jesus – Lord'.

Yet this word 'Lord' leaves us with one final issue for the integrity of faith. What of the future of this 'sojourn' by the 'sending' of the Son of Man? The Ascension was no forsaking and there is an 'abiding' in the 'body of Christ', the peoplehood of his indwelling. Will that suffice as the meaning of all that the incarnational 'episode' we have studied must embrace if he is Lord? The exaltation completes and achieves divine action in concern with revelation and grace. But what of final Lordship over the history into which he came? Ascension had made it no longer physical and, therefore, no longer historical in the once incarnational sense. 'Those wounds yet visible above' could only be said in that we now knew by them how the unchanging God had ever been and would for ever remain. But by his 'withdrawal' (in the terms the Incarnation had desired and known for their essential human-ness) there had come a genuine 'absentness' supervening on the very nature of that 'presence'. Had he really 'come' if he had not also 'gone' – not to annul or forego the condescension but to have us know its eternal fidelity in the other guise of the abiding Holy Spirit 'interpreting all things'.

What, however, of history's future as within that eternal fidelity in more than these interim terms of a Church faithful – or perhaps not – to that guiding 'Spirit of Christ'?

It is clear that, for some decades, the early Church awaited a return of Christ, as judge and lord, in 'like manner as they had seen him go' (Acts 1:11). But in what 'manner' had faith rightly 'seen him go' and why the order to cease 'gazing into heaven'? Not taking a 'physicality' there but leaving behind the divine meaning of a once-for-all incarnation, to 'abide with them forever'. It was hard to visualise how another 'descent' could be, in the due terms of 'power and glory'. In the very shape of its purpose, that first 'coming' had been as it were, a veiling, a kind of secrecy, in the unobtrusive character of birth. It was only poetic to say that 'simple shepherds knew that God had sent His son'. Nobody yet knew in those soundly ripe theological terms. The ultimate realisation would only come when the entire manhood story could be comprehended. Then narrative would tell it, as the beginning already containing the sequel and the climax – as contain them it clearly did. For without the antecedents no climax could have been. The Gospels and the Church became 'wise before the event' but only via their recognition through the whole.

How then to envisage an again descending Lord – the Lord they had now known him always to have been? How would the 'like manner' translate into the new idiom, given that the first idiom had been the shape of its intention in lowliness and humility, and be 'this same Jesus' differently?

In point of fact no further advent supervened. It is a deeply important fact that the early Church survived – rather we should say defied – the disappointment of the non-*parousia*, or 'appearing' of the risen Lord.

That situation might have been thought quite lethal to their confidence as to 'God in Christ', but it was not so. There was perplexity and anxiety, as with all occasions of 'hope deferred', seeing that the waiting and the negating are cumulative, while anticipation ebbs. 'Occupy till I come' stayed loyally in force. The Church sustained and widened its mission to the world. The eternal could not well be assessed in the measures of time. It had already – and momentously – acceded to them and the wonder sufficed, with the responsibility of love and ministry which it had bequeathed.

Yet futurity always fascinates with its yearning to be clarified, not least when divine fidelity might be in human doubt. The old question presents itself, as to Haggai and the re-builders of Jerusalem beyond the Exile: 'How do you see it now?' (2:3). How ought we now to see 'the advent hope'?

At least Haggai's precept: 'Be strong and work' will still be apposite, and stay the more so if we are described as those 'who love his appearing' (2 Timothy 4:8). The tidy schemes or forecasts of millenarians will not convince wise 'lovers'.

They are thrown back on the assurance they learned in 'Him who was' and constrained to carry it forward as also the truth of 'Him who is to come'. 'From this day to the ending of the world' was the proud confidence of a Shakespearean king, but he was only speaking on the eve of a battle which, he claimed, could prove it so. It is hard to envisage 'the ending of the world' in temporal sense. Perhaps by some collision with some vagrant massiveness hurtling out of space to do with us as once with dinosaurs. Or perhaps by some engulfment into war born of the clash of appetites and the wilfulness and greed and pain in global arrogance and deprivation, marshalling the techniques of a perverted science.

Whatever the scenario, it will – and it will not – have destroyed a sacramental earth, the earth which possessed and carried in experience the sacrament it constituted about Creator with creaturehood, about 'dominion' given and received. *Where* these were tenanted, enacted and fulfilled as their earth-bound, earth-had privilege will have 'ended', but *what* they meant, substantiated and found sacred is not so 'ended'. The word is ambiguous and covers both 'finish' and 'destiny', what is 'terminal' and what abides. 'The end is not yet' the impatient were warned: 'the end is not thus' uses the other sense of the word. 'Enduring to the end' in the first sense turns to 'enduring in the end' in the second, or, if we retain the temporal sense, 'enduring beyond the end'.

Out of the panorama of the centuries and the hazards of present time, can the advent meaning be other than this truth, for all time-reference, of a world, from start to finish, sacramental both in fact and experience? We have said that creation, creaturehood, in their mutual fitness, were divinely meant, still more divinely meant in Christ's redemption. All abide as never 'un-meant' in some differently understood 'end of time' or 'of the world'. They have consisted, thus far still consist, in the self-consistency of God, both Lord and Saviour. Faith about 'futures' then, personal and inclusive, stands in that consistency.

The element of judgement has always been present in that sense of hope. For the sacramental world, by the same token, meant trust and liability. These will not fail of reckoning. The meaning of 'the wrath of God' was never retributive or punitive in terms of violence or spite, but ever of reckoning about sacred trust. The sacredness that belongs means that the nemesis is within. By the same token the benediction of the faithful is no self-congratulation nor some arbitrary favour but the 'prospering of our handiwork' as 'the beauty – upon us – of the Lord our God'.

We live in a climate of the problematic. 'No problem' we say, quick with re-assurance. 'We have a problem' is how we concede perplexity and tell unease. Hope has always been of the problematic order. The very word commonly conveys how far it stays in doubt. It can only well survive in the company of 'faith and love', in the trio where Paul placed it. To know that the material/physical/temporal contains and furnishes the moral/spiritual/eternal means knowing it as sacramental and so doing is the central will of faith and the loyal practice of love. Hope has to belong with them. Horizons have a way of receding as we approach them. It is in their very nature.

Futures for the human scene cannot be of that order, unless the whole earth-placed experience of human meaning is 'an unsubstantial pageant fading'. Christian faith in its sacramental quality, as purposively created, divinely wanted and in Christ-terms loved, sees it truly 'substantial' in that very sacredness. Being thus more than temporal 'pageantry', eternal judgement, mercy and glory belong with its future whatever its temporal demise.

The Deuteronomist (29:29), in his reprospect and prospect for the people of Moses around the story of his death and unknown place of burial, had this wisdom to commend to them: 'Secret things belong to the Lord our God but the things that have been revealed belong to us and to our children for ever that we may observe and do all the words of this law'. Faith as to 'the Christian Jesus' has a similar confidence about the known reality of grace, the 'given' things of 'God in Christ', as containing and reserving things – belonging there – but withheld from us.

It may be countered that in Acts and early Letters, the New Testament is more than explicit about that *parousia*, the 'appearing' Christians were awaiting. The theme, however, was couched for them in terms which had to be understood in the realisation of a 'non-appearing' as expectation had awaited it. Accordingly, in out-living those first assumptions of faith, while living joyfully in its service, they had to read (or we have to read) the details that shaped the confidence in the sense agreeable to their hope's deferment.

Those details had to do with 'this same Jesus' – always and ever crucial – with 'in like manner'. In terms of the sovereignty the Ascension was affirming, 'a cloud received him out of their sight'. What obscures he enters and where he enters he reigns. 'Why stand ye gazing . . .' had point clear enough for any who were not lost in a cloud.

So they returned to Jerusalem, and to a Temple which for many symbolized the centre of the world, of the earth where God had planted His creation, had equipped and suited it for custodians with whom He could dwell, to Jerusalem scene of their direst failure, the very setting of a divine dwelling more His self-telling still, His presence in a babe in a manger and a man on a cross, 'the very flesh of His Word'. If the external world and humankind knew Him in 'the length and breadth' of 'grace and truth', 'One Lord Jesus Christ' would be their knowing 'in the depth and height'.

CHAPTER FIVE

According to the Scriptures

Paul's formula in 1 Corinthians 15:3 and 15:4 is pointedly echoed in the Creed known as Nicene and belongs squarely with the whole apostolic tradition with which he was at pains to align himself as 'one born out of due time' by anomalous recruitment 'en route to Damascus', so far from the Galilee of the duly called.

The phrase has the immediate prior meaning of the Hebrew Scriptures, the source book of prophetic precedent or the hints discerned in ancient psalmody. But it duly comes to mean for the heirs of Christian faith the Scriptures of Gospel portrayal and the Letters of apostolic correspondence gathered into the New Testament Canon. These became the book of reference for the self-understanding of the Church, its historic forming and its moral education. They were only coming into being when Paul coined that clause *kata tas graphas* that became the *secundum Scriptures* of the Latin Church, but they were destined to become the primary source of its self-understanding. So much was explicit in the very idea of the Canon.

We can imaginatively bring together these two 'accordings' by taking due note of the story in Luke 24, from verse 13, of the two disciples on the way to Emmaus on that 'third day'. It has often been surmised that they were man and wife, Cleopas and his lady. If so, it would be the more telling for the evident 'gender' co-operation in the early Church as clear from the Epistles.

But what 'day' was it? We must conjecture that Luke has – as it were – telescoped into dimensions of one 'day' what was, if not then factually certainly effectively, a more prolonged education into the two, abiding themes of Christianity – the sacramental meal and exegesis of the Scriptures. We have to note how in Luke's chronology the 'day' never 'ends' until the Ascension, which was, symbolically, forty days after Easter. Luke's narrative moves with its own momentum through the two returning to Jerusalem, group encounter with Jesus, their commission, more exegesis and the exit to Bethany and Jesus' finally leaving them, whereupon they return to the city and the Temple and the Gospel ends.

That sequence, if still a day, is surely a period-time. It can, therefore, assure us that 'according to the Scriptures' was a primary factor in the birth 'days' of the Church and their extended character.

There were many pressing reasons why it should be so. Jesus the Messiah, at the centre of their preaching, was the very nerve of their existence. Its veracity was no academic matter: its falsity would spell the end of them, in delusion and despair. It represented a verdict they had reached out of an abyss of direst failure, a morass of incomprehension and apparent cowardice for which they could only have a prostrating self-contempt.

Moreover, that verdict had to do with the utmost dissuasive, telling against its sanity and truth, namely crucifixion to which there surely attached a 'curse' damning all possibility of Messianic credibility. It was, we may say, the whole significance of the Resurrection that it should for ever lay to rest the logic in these monumental misgivings. Yet did it do so in such immediate terms when 'some doubted' and then 'a cloud received him out of their sight' and the immediate re-assurances ceased, could no longer be renewed? Part of the meaning of resurrection itself surely was a critical transformation of the craven into the confident, the broken into the resolute.

That story in their innermost souls needed to have recourse to how antecedent promise and precedent ought to be read, given how contentious anyway was that Messianic theme, how loaded with controversy the anticipations it kindled but too often left at issue. Jesus had 'fulfilled' them so dramatically – as their Gospel was learning to have it – that corroboration from revered but inconclusive texts was as urgent as it must be exacting.

Bearing crucially on this arduous situation was that they were a company of Jewish men and women undertaking to present their witness to their kindred 'people of the covenant'. It was vital that these should be persuaded out of their own sources, as being also those on which the apostolate rested and relied. The convincing of these and/or – later – the dissuading of their opposition meant that the issue between them, for good or ill, must betake itself to prophet and psalm and sift their hallowed wisdom. We have seen in Chapter Three how zealous the evangelists could be in their recruitment of texts, even in minute particulars, and sometimes with inventiveness.

The Nativity apart, it is noteworthy how many citations had to do with the Passion. For it was there the utmost contention revolved. It has been conjectured by some that perhaps there were already collections of texts to hand during Gospel writing, details from which may have affected the form of its narration of the Holy Week climax. If so the importance of events as 'fulfilments' was only the more underlined.

Echoes, however, of incidental data like that of Zechariah 12:10 in John 19:37 – 'a bone of him not broken' – are less important than the overall Hebraic sense of a humanity relevant to God, of divine commitment to 'a people', of 'mindfulness' coming to deliver, and of divine agency moving through human means – all these were deep in a theology and ready for the central vision of 'advent, suffering and glory'. So rooted was the conviction of a 'coming to deliver', that Luke in finding it Messianic could outflank the obvious question: 'Ought the Christ to suffer such things?' and turn it round so that he 'ought such things to suffer' as the very path taking him to glory. The credal theme of a 'descending and an ascending' was as old as Jacob's ladder.' That ready means of relation between 'above' and 'beneath' convinced him that the Bethel of his night's sojourn was indeed 'the house of God'.

There was still surer precedent for such divine encountering in the desert experience of Moses, with the call to liberate his people from Egypt. For what the voice told him in reassurance brought divine character and divine action into one in saying: 'I will be there as who there I will be.' What could be more apt to tell the meaning of the Creed concerning God in Christ? The event, but only when lived through, would be the revelation, Yahweh being in both, intending their unison and their import. The exegesis of Exodus 3:14 may seem subtle to the outsider but the drama of that liberation lay deep in the psyche of all Hebrews, one to which later crises of their history knew well to appeal. It perpetuated for them a sense of Yahweh as an activist from whom deeds might be expected, deeds that meant His coming and His caring.

It was this set of mind, patently, that lay behind the entire Messianic hope. 'The prosperity of His servant-people' (Psalm 35:27) being on His heart, how could their adversity, and tragedy, not also be? Indeed, for many a psalmist, as for the Isaiah of 53:10, 'prosperity' and 'Messiah' were almost synonymous terms. Hence their connection with an idealised Davidism and a 'sonship' to that royal master-mind of their Jerusalem.

For the disciples in their maturing into apostles (one of the great motifs of the New Testament) Jerusalem had become the supreme symbol of adversity, the tragedy of their Jesus crucified and of their own dark treason as his 'friends'. How then could they fail to see the central feature in the prophets' service to Messiah, namely the suffering they experienced? We saw earlier how 'the just had lived by their faith' and how 'faith had lived – had stood its ground – only by their fidelity'. Would Messiah then, in his identity – if ever identified – have that same quality, as one writer later told it, of being 'perfected through suffering'? Ought the, otherwise, overwhelming tragedy of Jesus' Cross to be interpreted in any other terms than those drawn from the Scriptures yielding these precedents?

According to Luke's narrative of the Emmaus road and of 'Scriptures at the table', Jesus himself used a form of words pointedly dismissing all doubt by reversing doubt's own question and asking faith's instead: 'Ought *not* the Christ to have suffered these things', that is 'the things' that had burdened all their exchanges as they walked by the way? Reliance on such precedent, as warrant for witness to what was perceived fulfilling it, was more than an instinctive feel for textual duty: it was a quest for inner integrity, made the more genuine by the strange measure of events and the late depth of perplexity and pain. Citation, which can so easily be the recourse of the lazy or the narrow of mind, was for these disciples becoming apostles the very crux of sincerity. They could recall their Master saying: 'You have heard it said, but I say to you . . .' quoting only to abrogate. Therefore, it was not on mere words they wanted to rely but on the solid precedents of deed and experience belonging – at whatever far remove – to 'men of like passion' with their Lord. Such were exactly to hand for them in the record of 'the goodly fellowship of the prophets', of sufferers for and with the truth whose relevance was not in word alone but in a narrative of life, of life unto death. It would be no accident that the ultimate doctrine of the Incarnation entailing the Cross would be formulated precisely in those terms and find its warrant from the compulsion of the ancient word.

The surest appreciation of 'according to the Scriptures' in this first retrospective sense is the study that traces its impact on the shape and content of the New Testament, that other – if uneasy – party to the unity of the Bible. There is a debt of imitation in the very idea that a 'collection' might be a 'Canon', a miscellany become the monitor of the community that engendered it.

Four Gospels, a cluster of Letters, a Book of Acts to join them and the mysterious text of 'Revelation to John of Patmos' were, to be sure, a collection markedly different from Law and history, psalmody and prophethood within the Hebrew Canon. In either case, they were eloquent of the ethos in their origins, the sanctions in their peoplehoods. These, more than the disparity in their time-range or the contrasts in their logics, are the clue to the tensions in having them one Bible.

The immediate point about the New Testament's rubric 'according to the(se) Scriptures' self-applied is that which understands why they exist at all, the factor in their coming to be. To have them in being at all is the sum of their significance. They were self-originating by reason of what they were required to narrate. The impulse to their textual existence was the dynamism in their story.

The three generating factors – given apostolicity *per se* – were a faith in the telling, an expanding community of believing, and a slow lapse of years. They were Scriptures which would not have been needed had their reality not existed – their reality that of Jesus being offered to the world. It is high irony that the teaching of Jesus – to which many have restricted his recoverable significance – owes its survival in any feasible detail – to his memory being cherished in terms far larger than moral education and to his 'memorabilia' (if we may so speak) being wanted in lands and by generations where they could only come by long-range report.

Thus the Gospels were needed, with time passing, because there were new initiates to their preached meaning who lacked acquaintance with their hinterland, receding as it was in years and belonging on a distant soil, while Epistles, fruit of the same double circumstance, undertook their pastoral nurture as the other realm of their initiation. The written documentation either way was thus entirely the product of mission. A Jesus his folk had not sought to take, qua Saviour, into the world, would not have survived to belong historically in any other capacity, his sermons finding record only in the bosom of his whole evangel and of custodians it moved into diaspora with his name. Mortal like all humans, their memories demanded the longer durability of pen and script.

Thus the Gospels came into being out of oral memory via a communal treasury of mind and recitation and discourse, into acquiring an 'according to Scripture' status – a process doubtless attended by many vicissitudes. Their out-of-mission origin is underlined by passage out of Aramaic into Greek, and that – for the most part – by Jewish hands and in care of the thoroughly Jewish theme of divinely accomplished action in 'Messiah according to Jesus'. Dramatic in itself, that language transition could be read as Jewish vocation fulfilled by 'Gentile' inclusion.

So much in the *raison d'être* of the New Testament Letters belongs in the pastoral liabilities of that transition. The 'pearls before swine' metaphor lingered, reportedly, from Jesus himself. Folk rawly out of paganism were dubiously ready for the precious disciplines of the morally circumcised. The 'suspected' on that score needed to understand their 'newness of life' in Christ, while the 'suspicious' deserved the steady re-assurance of their scruples about the new inclusions. It would be fair to say that the apostolic Letters were the Church's moral discovery of itself, or active tuition in self-identity as 'people of God'.

That the task was painstakingly undertaken is evident from the range of matters handled – sexual license and litigious partisanship in Corinth, gnostic vagaries in Colosse, impetuous superstition in Galatia, wild expectation in Thessalonica and loss of heart among readers of 1 Peter. All these could become part of what 'according to Scriptures' would yield, of precedent and guidance, for centuries to come. Only the Philippians seem to have merited only commendation, while the more treatise-like tuition of Romans and Ephesians could serve no less aptly for education of a long future. All apostolic writing might thus be likened to a smithy in which was forged the armoury of 'the good fight of faith', the immediacy of brief defining years and action making the guide-book of the long future, life educating life in a legacy of script.

That scope and world of the Epistles was the matrix of the Gospels which, for the most part, the Letters preceded. It has sometimes been argued that the Epistles betray little interest in the person and the career of Jesus of Nazareth. It is a curious charge, given the extensive citation of his words and steady reference to his example. Indeed his Passion is at the very centre of the Christian living the Letters teach and enjoin. 'Let this mind be in you which was also in Christ' is the ground rule of all. What is true is that the Letters 'tell' Christ inside their own task of devotion and nurture in the churches of dispersion and do so – we must assume – in the knowledge that instincts, moving apace, were cherishing and assembling the 'gospels to be' with their kindred, but different, purpose of a Jesus-history.

'The mind of Christ' – we might say – informing Christian living was the caring role of the Letters, 'the mind of Jesus' informing the story of his Christhood being the quest of the Gospels. Each was essentially part of the other, but in necessary dual shape, in the exigencies of a growing and dispersing community which called, through the same years, for a grasp on its origins *and* a grasp on the direction of its life. Both tasks were truly apostolic – what we live by and how we live by it, the light in which we walk and our walk in that light.

Again, obvious dispersion is a primary factor in either case – the one becoming many, and the many somehow remaining one. Diversity, whether of locale, or speech, or culture, is both the stimulus and the threat to unity. Paul's Letters breathe oxygen from the one and struggle with the other. They are only bravely exemplary of a perpetual task. The Gospels, for their part, are about where unity derives in the one Jesus but in being four they align diversity, not in lacking a consensus verdict but in reaching it with individual emphases. These, however, especially as between the three and the fourth, can be most tellingly unified. The immediate point is to know the New Testament as 'consensual' in its witness to 'the original Jesus' understood as found and told in the society believing he had originated it. Hence its Letters, hence its Gospels, serving sufficiently to underwrite their issue from him and their status for him as what only community could have sufficed to shape and, in so doing, owe itself entirely to him.

It follows that any 'according to the Scriptures', meaning the Church's confidence in them, and case-making from them, is evidently a 'faith from faith', in that it validates itself by what it has itself brought about, namely text concerning theme. That, however, does not make it a 'faith in faith' – a charge with which the following chapter has to deal. The situation has to be held inside the concept of a presiding 'Holy Spirit', as 'guiding into truth'.

That the Gospels are 'faith from faith' is evident enough from their very shape and selectivity and even – we might say – from their incompleteness, as angles of vision not their own might think to allege. That Passion narratives are prior in them and that they are not 'lives of Jesus' are features often noted. Teaching and suffering are integral to each of them. Just as they need and wait for 'exegesis', so they are themselves their 'exegesis' of their Jesus. Their faith is finding him this way because this way he found or earned their faith. So much John 1:18 tells us in playing on the verb *exegesato*. 'The Word made flesh' exegetes the Father, 'interprets' to the world the divine nature. Of this living exegesis the Gospels are the 'interpreter', and from our 'reading' of them we reach to both.

Those Gospels, then, are conducers to belief out of their own induction into it by him who was 'in the bosom of the Father'. Thus John 20:31 writes of the whole text's existence as being 'in order that you made hold the faith that Jesus in the Christ', or 'that you may come to believe his Messiahship'. Similarly, Luke introduces his Gospel as designed to present 'the things most surely believed among us'.

It was noted earlier, in Chapter Four, that all the Gospels derive from commitment to faith seeing that, otherwise, they would not exist. They address outsiders because they belong with insiders. Impartiality would disqualify their character – a situation which is the very shape of their integrity. They can only confirm faith by awakening it. Their being is to be received.

There is a reasoned consensus about a commanding concern for Jesus' teaching but a profound issue around how that concern emerges in the Fourth Gospel. The debt of all three Synoptic Gospels to a corpus of cherished sayings of Jesus (labelled 'Q' from *quelle*, a source) squares with the sense of a communal treasury of oral memory implicit in the very nature of the Church. All three employ it while Matthew organizes much of it in formal *didache*, or teaching, as if to read Jesus as a new Moses, albeit speaking with an 'I say unto you' and not from a height of Sinai – a contrast of deliberate significance. A number of parables are common to all three though none recognizably survive in John where some have allusive echoes in the different Johannine world. Luke has a precious body of teaching and parable unique to himself and in line with his feel for the being universal of divine salvation – a feature basic to his nativity inaugural.

Only he and Matthew choose to begin with birth. Mark has 'the beginning of the Gospel' (1:1) as 'Jesus came preaching', an immediate sequel to 'the baptism of John' the preluding baptizer. The evangelist John, as his text now stands, has that crucial figure abruptly set ('there was a man sent from God whose name was John') inside the profoundest theology of his, otherwise, wholly discursive Prologue brooding on divine Self-giving.

All four Gospels culminate in Passion narrative in direct nexus with the teaching, healing ministry from which the crisis stemmed. Each traces in its distinctive terms, the drama of encounter which Jesus underwent at the hands of an 'establishment' of authority and tradition. In this quality, they were also reflecting the experience of the churches in their dispersion in a world where Jewish diaspora was well able, and often minded, to renew what that encounter had first concerned.

Such was the continuity of inner logic from the things at issue about Jesus in Galilee and Jerusalem to those at stake in the confession of him by the Church. If Messiahship had deserved rejection in the one, it could hardly have peaceable recognition in the other's witness to it. The point is crucial for a query that is always close at hand around the integrity of the New Testament. It has to do with where Paul, the great evangeliser, belongs with these Gospels of the four evangelists. He is often accused – only ignorantly – of himself ignoring them as preoccupied only with his version of a saving Christ whose sermons he could well neglect. The notion is a travesty. For were it true neither he, as this Paul, nor these, as Gospels, would exist. Both belonged only from an essential coherence between them, seeing that Paul's conversion – and his implementation of its meaning in his wide evangelism – derived from the entire significance of the Passion as the Gospels told it. The antipathy he encountered turned on the same point as the condemnation of Jesus. Paul's whole career is thus bound existentially into the history writing the four Gospels comprise. His involvement with diaspora could resign to these the onus of telling the story that had taken him to 'the nations'. The Gospels would sufficiently explicate what had made him an apostle while he fulfilled that making of him.

That way, faith may detect a double, unitary, 'exegesis' of Jesus – the one in a textual scripture, the other in a venture into mission. It was, therefore, proper that the two should combine into a single volume – not as apostolic biography, for their *raison d'être* had only the one life-source in

Jesus – but as that source translating from where it had belonged to where it would extend. The Gospels and the apostle Paul were differently serving the same intention present in the Incarnation. What Paul in his letters cares about autobiographically only figures there as illuminating the theme in his mission. His service never displaces his Lord. Rather it offers a sort of commentary on the Gospel from inside its own errand in the world.

Hence the feasibility of Luke writing his 'Acts of Apostles' as coupled into one 'book' with his Gospel. The linking of two texts – for all its problems for the scholars – symbolises this bonding of Gospel-writing with Gospel-travelling and Luke himself a party in the first and a partial companion in the second. Aside from conjectures around that symbol, it is clear that there is a presence of diaspora experience in the fabric of the Gospels as they take shape in their community-formation. This is so not only in the sense already noted of a constituency awaiting them, but as containing matters impinging on local situations, themes acquiring interest, and perhaps even inclusion, for their relevance to daily life. For the churches with their Jew/Gentile tensions, their Christian/pagan neighbouring, reproduced, in some measure, what obtained between Jesus and his immediate Palestinian audience. In documenting the latter, evangelists, immersed in the communities for which they wrote and from which they drew their vocation, could hardly escape the former.

What, for example, was to be drawn from the episode about an 'elder brother' not going in to share the feast of the 'prodigal's return', in Luke's most famous parable? Was the family Jewish? Luke does not specify and mostly parables have no ethnic discrimination. So the story just has to do with a rather cold, legal-minded self-righteousness not recognising any genuine worth in wayward penitence? That might well be, but – given communities where recent 'Gentiles' were to be welcomed with joy and where continuing Jews, or perhaps newly Christian ones, could not countenance such warmth of unity but held aloof – did Luke's parable assume a larger, and differently contentious, meaning? Could the simple preaching's concern with penitence from Jesus' place and time embrace this wider relevance from decades on?

That all the Gospels antedate what they postdate is evident enough – unless seeing it so is refused by a false notion of Biblical loyalty. The inclusion of 'the great commission', there and then in Mark and Matthew and, in Matthew's, the citation of the Trinitarian formula of 'baptism in the Name of the Father, the Son and of the Holy Spirit', are – as the term goes – there and then 'proleptic'. It is clear that the 'commission' was being obeyed long before it was formalised in those terms, terms that took time to come to credal language. It is not that Mark and Matthew falsify. In truth they had that mandate. The very going in it would allow it to be finalised in credal words. Words were, therefore, truly linked with its narration, just as it would be true to say that the author of *Romeo and Juliet* wrote *Hamlet* so becoming the Shakespeare he always was. The truth of the Trinity was there in latency before it told itself in formal words and creed.

Thus the Gospels always have to be studied with a kind of bifocal vision, alert to what is before in incidence and after in interpretation. In some measure all historiography is that way.

Nowhere is this matter of the time-set of the Gospel's story and the view-point of its telling more central than in the Fourth, the Gospel according to John. Here, 'according to the Scripture', this text that became Scripture, has a weight as radical factor that many readers have been unable or unwilling to understand. This Gospel has a quite unique proleptic character in that how the evangelist sees Jesus is so thoroughly responsive to an incarnational theology as to transform the portraiture as becomes a different figure. Yet right analysis cannot too firmly insist that, in so doing, John writes a gospel. So emphatically is this so, that sharp historical contours present themselves, like the one already noted in the midst of the Prologue about 'a man sent from God', so prosaically factual.

John's Gospel is not a treatise, nor an essay in philosophy though it has features that resemble these. It is thoroughly located in people, events, times and places as these belong in the Synoptics – sometimes more precisely than with them and putting chronology squarely to the test. Yet its Jesus moves more enigmatically, speaks more unfamiliarly and acts more magisterially than elsewhere in them, or they show such Johannine features rarely, hardly at all, or they only have them implicitly in their much more congenial and mutual *mise-en-scène*.

To register the contrasts is to realise that we cannot have the synoptic Jesus *and* the Johannine Jesus by any easy reconciliation, still less let the contrasts lie unexamined as if non-existent or 'signifying nothing'. For they 'signify' enormously and taking them intelligently is a duty to all four Gospels. In John Jesus does not parabolise, he 'signals' or symbolises. Occasions of healing, far fewer on his canvas, develop into discourses which turn them into 'signs'. These are not points of recruitment, as often elsewhere, but rather evidences of failure to understand or of need for wiser discernment. Jesus, for his part, 'did not trust himself' to 'those who saw the signs he performed' (2:24). His works had to do with the terms in which he wished to be believed. While 'evidences' mattered as 'credentials', he disparaged the facile 'faith' they might arouse (4:48, 20:29). John, in his Letters too, is interested in people 'being in the truth'; he is preoccupied about 'apostate-hearers'.

Alert readers of the Fourth Gospel are at once aware of a strong authorial handling of the contents and how they are arranged around a sequence
of 'signs' and, indeed, a sequence of interviews. The interviews can be read
as representative of what is at stake between himself and 'official Jewry'
(not Jewry *per se*). What are, in Mark, Matthew and Luke, clashes about
the Sabbath, law as rigour and Yahweh as 'compassion' and rabbinical
teaching authority, become in John still more pointed and contentious.
We have to take account of the hardening that ensued in the dispersion
where, after the Fall of Jerusalem, Jewish Christians would 'be expelled
from the synagogue' (9:22). Is John transposing one context or scenario
to another and doing so intelligibly, in that the 'present' knew the 'future
of that past'?

His authorial liberty is extensively at work in this time-shift sense. How
otherwise, in 1:29, could he have John the Baptist introducing 'two disciples' (Andrew and another) to Jesus as 'the Lamb of God', Andrew whom
Jesus called at the seaside? If, in the beginning of their story, they had been
told of Jesus *in those terms*, how could they have been so uncomprehending all the way to the Cross itself?

Here was the 'proleptic' indeed. The Baptist's ministry was prior to
Andrew's discipleship and the one he followed *came to be* for him in truth
'the Lamb of God'. So, there and then, at the first call, it was 'the Lamb'
he followed but would only – and at length in the following – come to
know as such. Only as implicit in the long event was it there at the start.

So much in John is of this order. Committed to his theme of confronta-
tion, implicit from the outset, John can have the cleansing of the Temple
there in Chapter Two, while the factual, the synoptic, timing is a climax
at the end. To assume on John's part this creativity of presentation is more
intelligent than to surmise that there were two cleansings. Or one might
do so only in a forfeiture of the high drama of the second – the drama
John keeps in his strategy, having the immediate sequel in 2:18–22 remi-
niscent of Passover time in Matthew 26.

What is noteworthy in this and many other passages in John is the
comment about how, afterwards, 'the disciples remembered . . .'. He
betrays his vantage-point in 'the future of the past'. He is not unmindful
of chronology in being so insistently thematic. He tells of disciple-recruit-
ment and moves to a detailed Passion climax. He is also careful about
Hebrew Festivals and links his meanings to them. So much is this the case
that some scholars have surmised that he builds his authorial scheme
around a Jewish Lectionary, perhaps to point his vision of Jesus as the
fulfilment of the whole Jewish liturgy of celebration and recital. Several
discourses find their thrust from motifs in the feast days or from the synagogue readings that went with them. Perhaps the 'shepherd' imagery of

John 10 belongs with the 'shepherd readings' of Genesis 46 and 47 going with the Feast of the Dedication, or Ezekiel 34 with its indictment of criminal shepherds.

Perhaps, however, we may borrow clues to John's skill with evangel from a much wider field, even from the likes of the Greek historian Thucydides or other classical writers. The idea of any parallel has to be pondered with caution. Certainly they sought to convey how situations belonged with personalities by letting these speak from inside their actual response to them, in speeches that could never have been 'recorded' in their sequence but nevertheless 'conveyed' the essence of the actual scene more tellingly than any bare chronicle of inarticulate deeds. Words were only set on their lips because what they carried was *in* the history as transacted in their hearts. The historian's authorship of them had, thereby and without any treachery, the more effectively told their meaning and significance. Likewise, Virgil in his vivid personalising of the founding of Rome.

John, as evangelist, has a very different vocation, but what the close student perceives him doing is not utterly dissimilar, only that, rather than history being made realist, we have in John the ultimate made contemporary. By his time of writing, Jesus, in the faith-experience of the Church, has become the 'divine visitant' from heaven – in the 'visitation' that had verily (a favourite word) transpired in Galilee and Jerusalem. Either was integral to the other. Could he, therefore, tell the historically actual speaking the eternal content and do so, by having Jesus, in the given context of the first, use the language of the second? The historical was where that content belonged, though then unrecognised yet, none the less, its inner quality.

There would be no falsehood in doing so. The 'where' was valid and the 'who' was its meaning, only that it was a 'fullness' which, in the actuality of a 'temporal' in an 'eternal' would await recognition only when recognition would be found, namely in the fruition faith had in the sequel the Church would be to it and because of it.

So John has Jesus speaking as 'the eternal Word', in terms that would be incomprehensible otherwise. Synoptic narrative of the bread broken among the congregation in the plain affords setting for a discourse about 'living bread from heaven' with the then distant yet now familiar liturgy where 'my flesh is meat indeed'. Times conflated are one with situations merged. Only thinking figuratively about the sacrament would consist rightly with appreciating literally the satisfied hunger of the historic crowd.

There are many such loaded situations in John's narrating a theology and theologising a narrative. Interviews with individuals, like Nicodemus and the Samaritan woman at the well, merge into discourses quite contrasted with the parables elsewhere. The interview of Jesus with his visitor 'by night' seems informed by a later perspective on how Jewish interest in 'the Christian Jesus' had to reckon with 'new birth' for all and on how difficult Jews would find it – not a situation so evident in those terms in the Synoptics. The well of Sychar, too, seems to be reflecting a situation where new people became their own evangelists and could say: 'We have heard him ourselves . . .' – a natural progress given the lapse of time.

But, more important than these implications from diaspora experience, is the dilemma New Testament exegesis has about having 'the same Jesus' between the four Gospels except by resolving the disparities inside the faith in the Incarnation as intelligently inclusive of them, seeing that only so are they honestly compatible. That there should be 'one and the same Jesus' is crucial to all else in Christian faith, whether about humanity in creation or credibility in God. Having it so, however, must face how deep the inter-Gospel contrasts go. We cannot blandly have them both ways and will lose vital truths if we wish to assert what we do not examine.

Nowhere is the issue more pointed than in narratives of Gethsemane. Where is the anguished Jesus of 'Let this cup pass from me,' and 'great tears of blood falling . . .' (Luke 22:44) in the supremely confident figure in John 17? Or, where the drowsy, broken disciples in 'I have given them Thy Word and they have known . . .' (John 17:14 and 8)? In either case, it is the same Gethsemane. Can both perceptions be right, unless the Johannine one is understood as retroactively perceiving the synoptic crisis in the terms it would have – and therefore *did* essentially have – of resurrection faith?

John 17 reads, tremendously, as a final 'testament', a summation of the entire achievement of 'the Word made flesh'. It glows with the theme of 'glory' – the theme that is at the heart of all we are exploring, the 'glory' that burns in the tragic only because it is the nature of the victory. It has the Johannine Christ celebrate the Galilee/Gethsemane Jesus on his own lips. Its refrain of past tenses – 'I have given . . .' 'they have known . . .' 'I have manifested . . .' 'they have kept . . .' inaugurates a series of present ones – 'now I come to Thee . . .' 'these are in the world' which pass, in turn, into prayer about continuity, unity and sanctity. The whole is a hymn of glad prospect grounded in accomplished retrospect, a 'seeing by a man of sorrows the travail of his soul' and crying: 'satisfied.' John has it where it belongs. The reader must do no less, noting too how 'this eminently Christian Jesus' (such as the passage finds him) even sets something like an early creed on his own tongue, where he becomes – as it were – a third party in the clause:

> This is life eternal – that they might know Thee, the only true God and Jesus
> Christ whom Thou hast sent. (17:3)

There could be no clearer witness to the faith of the Church entering into the discourse of Jesus and set deep in the immediate history, this Gethsemane, where the faith had its origin.

Thus the genius behind the Johannine text gives us the assuring way through our reading task between the Gospels. The Father 'glorifies' the Son; the Son 'glorifies the Father' – in the mutual divine conspiracy as the human 'visitation', the 'coming' to reveal and save, the 'leaving' that would abide ever in the meaning left as a trust this divine condescension would continue to guide and enable. 'These are Thine for Thou gavest them to me . . . keep them through Thy word.'

We need, then, have no final misgiving about 'the same Jesus'. The more immediate, down-to-earth, topical narration of Mark, Matthew and Luke, far from being foreign to it, is kindred with the theology of the story that finds itself in the mind of John thinking with the ascended Christ. Indeed those three are not lacking in notes of John's music. We really need our Johannine Jesus to have one inviting all the world of the weary to 'rest in his yoke', or one aware of 'all things delivered to him by the Father', as to 'the Son who alone knows Him' (Matthew 11:25–30).

The distinctive sense of a Jesus-in-Christology which has perhaps its sharpest focus in his chapter 17 extends, if with less intensity, to all else in his handling of, or neglect of, what is in the Synoptics. It belongs with his selectivity, his organising of works of mercy into 'seven signs', perhaps in line with Judaic symbolism, his deepening of questions of law and authority into issues of theology, his heightened concern about the implications for ongoing Judaism of any 'Christian Jesus'. Hence the prominence he gives to Messianic identification in conflict with Jewish leadership, as an issue more theoretical at stake than in the synoptic ministry, where it was more implicit than explicit, in the necessary reservations of Jesus about publicity. Throughout, indeed, Jesus 'could not be hid', but by John's sights the open question had passed into a differently public domain, given the hardening of Judaic attitudes reciprocal to the growth of the institutional and partly 'Gentile' Church. Thus the synoptic ministry of Jesus is perceived through the corporate life of a new 'people under God'.

In the same context we can understand how the sacramental principle of Eucharist blends, in John's chapter 6, with the practical quality of 'bread among so many' in a 'desert place'. Even so, there is something anticipatory in 'making the men sit down' and having the disciples such crucial agents in an orderly distribution. In this way, things synoptic are anticipatory of things Johannine, but only by dint of the emergence anyway of the faith-community that has grown out of the one in becoming the other. What things were was not just in the way they once happened but in the life-pattern they had found for themselves – both thanks only to Jesus. What was first incident in a story comprises what is now present in the churches, as antecedence and consequence. Things are foreshadowed, to be later realised. John links them in numerous ways. 'Other sheep I have . . . them also I must bring' (10:16) enlarges the original meaning of 'the shepherd of Israel'. The Church's mission in their 'bringing' is more surely understood from discussion elsewhere about worship detached from Jerusalem's Temple, to which the conversation led in John 4:20–23.

If, by 3:13, Jesus is still in conversation with Nicodemus (we do not know where the discourse ends) he is already ascended, being 'the Son of man who is in heaven'. Two realms are clearly fused – the interview and the theology as one voice speaking. What should we make of 'because I was with you' (16:4), said to them when ostensibly he is also still with them? There are many such 'bi-focal' allusions to a present-past in the richly devotional passages of John's chapters 14 to 16. Is it that, for John, the ascended Christ is speaking as still the historic Jesus? If so, the evidence is clearer than ever that he writes a narrative Gospel only to offer a Gospel theology.

That future-in-present perspective seems confirmed, for example, by the curious question in 7:35: 'Will he go into the diaspora among the Greeks and teach the Greeks?' In the Synoptics the ministry is strictly confined. Is there an insinuation about one likely to do better among 'Gentiles' than amid Jerusalem's Jewry – an oddly perceptive gibe (unwittingly) since John's Jesus was referring to his Ascension, 'the suffering and the glory' which would have precisely that pro-'Gentile' sequel. At least John writes from a perspective which includes that dimension.

It has been vital for our being 'accordant to the Scriptures', to give sustained attention to the nature of the Fourth Gospel but only for the integral witness of the four. The negligence of not doing so would take toll of our sanity and honesty. For there have been those, out of incomprehension, who have read the Fourth Gospel as 'changing a Galilean teacher into the God who goes about on earth'. Such have seen omnipotence walking around pretending to be otherwise and, in John, we can see it, and see through it, most obviously.

Christology, in those terms, fails lamentably of due and sane comprehension. The secret, so evident in John, is totally forfeit. It lies in the lowliness of which Mary sang in her Magnificat which, being known in the instrument was all the more truly found in the fulfilment. 'In the midst of the throne the Lamb slain.' The theme of the 'glory' was – and is – the majesty of the self-given, 'the Christ in God' as from 'the God in Christ'.

New Testament faith is saying that we do not have our theology except with the Christology it essentially possesses. Its surest statement is the Johannine Prologue so memorably fusing the two '. . . ologies' together via the commanding word of creation becoming the 'dwelling' Word of Incarnation. It cherishes the ancient imagery of 'tentedness', of 'the tabernacle of God being with humanity', the *eskenosen* of John 1:14, 'habiting among us' in the double purpose of revelation and redemption, divine Self-expression as – by the same token – divine Self-fulfilment.

Or, if not the tent imagery among us nomads, then the man-reality this 'tabernacle' always was, as we can readily take from a perhaps unusual suggestion, where there is a haunting kinship of mind between the Hebraic and the Christian around the analogy of 'shepherd', so beloved in either Testament. Numbers 27:16–17 reads:

> Let the Lord, the God of the spirits of all flesh, set a man over the congregation, who will go out before them, and who may lead them out and who may bring them in, that the congregation of the Lord are not as sheep who have no shepherd.

The man so appointed was named Joshua. Another one, explicitly so named, echoed that ending phrase about the reason and the need.

> When he saw the multitude, he was moved with compassion on them, because they fainted and were scattered abroad as sheep that had no shepherd. (Matthew 9:36)

Whatever the urgent Christian misgivings about that first Joshua with his ethnic cleansings, there is no escaping the pathos in the refrain and the compassion and the human plight. According to Isaiah 53:6, we recognise in them the truth of ourselves.

Faith in Jesus, then, as the Incarnate Lord, is just this divine compassion initiated by 'the God of the spirits of all flesh' and transacted among them in 'the Word made flesh' 'bringing them in' to the experience of grace where 'God and Word' as one 'dwell among us' in the very truth of a divine compassion. Thus, then, the historic faith about 'the Christian Jesus', the divine drama from 'beyond' to us 'down here', the advent through to an ascension and all between – these are the 'mercy from on high' to where 'out of the depths we cry' to have it so.

'Remembrance' is the hallmark of the New Testament – remembering 'the promise' from far generations, 'remembering that he had spoken these things unto them', 'doing this in remembrance of him', and through the

Spirit 'bringing all things to remembrance', the words with 'the Word', and 'He more likest God in being born'.

This confidence that lives in present tense is by no means at an end of questions, not least with John and, for example, how we should understand the raising of Lazarus and the strange silence of the Synoptics concerning him, as some conclusive 'sign of resurrection' when he would shortly die again and when Jesus had so distrusted faith turning only on surprise or spectacle. Some of the disputanda come in the chapter to follow.

That would not be faith which was attended by entire or incontestable proof. Convictions beyond interrogation would not deserve the name. It suffices that there is a way to go and a commitment to accept. Our grasp is there within our reach and 'God – this way – in Christ' invites them both.

In preface to our next task, it remains to ask whether a faith that requires such careful exegesis by its faithful can readily fit a world so far unready or unable to bring that requisite? It is not implied that only sophisticates believe. Others do so deeply. Yet through the ages of faith an easy literalism has had great attraction and led to much sanguine and unseemly believing, if not to sorry superstition. 'The text says' too often pre-empts as an instinct what 'the text means' as its true concern. 'According to the Scriptures' is, therefore, a rubric for reference but also for discrimination. What 2 Timothy 2:15 calls 'rightly dividing the word of truth' is a caring and a taxing art, a skill proper to the reading that interprets because it was needed in the transaction this must have with the setting where it started.

Hence the steady reliance we must have on the Holy Spirit whom textual Scriptures never supersede in the ordering of the personal or the ecclesial mind. There is no text that can make our duty obsolete. Between that Holy Spirit and ourselves security is had in letting an advent and an ascension, and all they made ours between, 'establish our hearts in the knowledge and love of God', and let all else be ruled inside that trust.

CHAPTER SIX

Disputanda

St. Mary's, the University Church of Oxford, has memories of many contrasts in high points of history and numberless acts of private meaning. Within its walls Thomas Cranmer made his famous recantation of a recantation in the burdened reign of Mary. Three centuries later, Matthew Arnold described the strange influence over its crowded pews of the famed eloquence, the mystical piety, of John Henry Newman's sermons. Historians find themes inside its story and theologians no less. So also might a wistful agnostic, local known or casual alien, find impulse there as 'serious house on serious earth'.

One occasional frequenter in that non-worshipping capacity was the much esteemed, prolific novelist and tough philosopher, Iris Murdoch. Her long friend and recent biographer tells us:

> She might occasionally be seen standing in the back of St. Mary's, for she could never entirely leave Christianity, though she could never embrace the myths of the Virgin Birth and the Resurrection.

Peter Conradi kindly avoided the loaded word 'swallow' in reference to those often unpalatable 'myths', which – if in trite, vulgar usage of the word – those two dissuasives about Christianity are held to be.

Iris Murdoch, with her Ulster antecedents and her Oxford reputation, is one from whom we may fitly start on 'disputanda' concerning Christian faith – and the better so as one who, like her contemporary, the poet Philip Larkin, would perhaps have 'liked to' believe but scrupulously could not. Christians have no quarrel with the scruple. They know the duties themselves, if they are honest, though not the instinct to think they point in only one direction. Murdoch is an arch-exponent of the view that religious faith is a futile quest for a consolation in the human world which does not and cannot exist.

> When other helpers fail and comforts flee
> O Thou who changest not abide with me . . .

would be her *bête noire*. 'Other helpers fail' and always will. Oddly, for this view, it is not that humans lack relevance – a relevance that reaches beyond themselves. For she has a very central and powerful role for ethics. Hers is by no means a morality-free society nor a meaningless world. This emphatic relevance, however, about her existence, an authentic liability for the beings we are and the risks we carry, is not allowed to argue any ground or *raison d'être* for its being so outside a human creation of it. Emphatically, 'we are on our own'. There *is* a moral ultimacy – and there must be to give mandatory occasion to values and criteria of behaviour to which we are utterly accountable. This 'not-ourselves', however, (not ourselves in its warrant to require its due from us) has no 'not-ourselves' counterpart – as theism believes – as ever relevant by way of grace and aid, or even illumination, on our performance. There is no relevance *outside* ourselves *for* the relevance in ourselves that might avail *to* ourselves – what, in its own word, Christianity calls salvation.

So, we are on our own even in the acknowledgement of claims and values that, for their being in no way whimsical, are certainly over us. We do not well anticipate, however, anything 'over us' in a morally enabling sense.

Is there not a trace of sour grapes about this veto on consolation, if not in Iris Murdoch, with her many probing explorations of the human condition? Do we need to begin from a basic suspicion about who and where we are in the wideness of the world? It would seem churlish and darkly reductionist to do so, neutralising the potentialities inviting us to engage. Nature and human nature seem to relate both ways, suggesting an arena as the one and a guesthood as the other. Childhood from the outset, if not warped by adversity, assumes a context that signifies and will respond and for which there is no instinctive distrust. The infant smile, it has been noted, is the beginning of language, prior to all words, yet conveying what awaits them.

Unbelief, like belief too, is for large part a matter of the will. Thus Murdoch writes in her *The Sovereignty of Good*:

> That human life has no external point or *telos* is a view as difficult to argue as its opposite and I shall simply assert it. I can see no evidence to suggest that human life is not something self-contained . . . Our destiny can be examined but it cannot be justified or totally explained. We are simply here. (London, 1970, p. 79)

Theologians, for the most part, have not willed 'merely to assert' their contrary view. For the careful, persistent, mental efforts of theology fathered centures ago perceptions of order and significance inside human experience which for long tutored and inspired philosophy itself to think expectantly of metaphysics. The word 'totally' in the foregoing might leave a glimmer of hope that 'examined destiny' might perhaps prove a less forlorn goal to contemplate. Either way 'truth cannot become true till faith has made it so'. Given any will to venture faith-wise, latent 'evidence' may become more visible and give pause to 'self-containment'. Or, if we are talking about 'courage to thank whatever gods there be', for 'an unconquerable soul', such brave heroes have no lonely lease on it. There is a deep but quieter courage in much gentle faith. One is not a believer merely out of some reluctance to look into the void.

It seems odd on Murdoch's part to have characters talk about 'concealing the absence of God' – which is what, on her view, religion contrives to do. Either an 'absence' is itself a 'concealment' which could be 'presented' by revelation, or there was no 'absentee' to 'conceal' because of authentic tokens of a presence.

That tokens discerned in the external world as significant to our being human and potentially fulfilling us, is a basic assumption of all science in its acceptance of the material world. How then we accept and judge the liability-to-be as it derives from this inter-est between intelligibility there around us and our intelligence with it, is, of course, the question at the heart of even secular morality. It deepens into what begins to be religious when that 'ethical', perhaps by way of beauty but more by awe and wonder, conveys us to a sense, however thus far tentative, of a situation proving to be reciprocally personal.

Personhood on the human side is certainly where and how the situation registers, being critical, sensory, mental, physical and – through all these – spiritual. Automata would not know it so. May what is already mutual by all those adjectives allow us to suspect, if not also to believe, that the 'personal' which embraces them, is also mutual? This may be far from crying with a Biblical assurance: 'O God, Thou art my God', but – depending on how forthcoming that transcendent 'personal' may be – a cry we may one day learn to use.

So all turns on the forthcoming-ness. Need it be one we wilfully forbid, exclude, deride or otherwise take out of reckoning? To be sure, we need circumspection, alert to proclivities that are merely ours and conduce to idol-making or illusion. In our sort of world we will never lack the cautioners, who must never, however, deny us the 'grand perhaps' by which faith lives until it can assure itself of 'One who is'.

In that way all intelligent theism argues from the same human self-scrutiny as any alert agnosticism, namely the sense every selfhood knows of 'being', of 'being here' and – however we sift it for reasons and for policy – of 'being liable', so that our selfed-situation, even if being deplored or un-desired, cannot be dismissed. For dismissal would be dire action with it. Buddhism, too, begins with this self-reality and proposes a strategy of 'undesiring'. 'Not being', then can only be an option 'being' takes about a selfhood that is ineluctable, since – clueless or clue-given – we are here. Believing ourselves clue-given in this capacity to assess ourselves will be no less reasonable than to think ourselves clue-denied.

Any clue-given verdict will imply a clue-giver, a source in our 'being desired', that might be reciprocal to the 'desire' we find implicit in our sheer existence and at issue in our selfhood. That such a 'meantness' about us is credibly discernible is, of course, the whole point of the theme of 'creation' as argued in Chapter Two. That we are free to doubt it is no small part of its generosity, so that acceding to be 'creatures', and neither 'gods' nor 'puppets', recognises how being 'clue-given' invites into the exploration of the world, into a relationship of liability in the natural order and an economic management of the 'dominion' this affords.

Thus we are free to read – or at liberty not to read – this positive relevance in whom and where and how we are and reach for that beyond it which contrived it so. Such theism has the right to be tentative and, therefore, friendly with the unpersuaded, seeing that all is in the nature of an invitation, an intimation saying: 'Seek and ye shall find.' If, as already, we are talking of some forthcoming-ness responsive to our urgency, there must be a greeting for it of our own. There, perhaps, is where much agnosticism stumbles. It will not be uprighted by what does not sympathise with its hesitancy.

Where, and how, then, might we anticipate this divine forthcoming-ness before we ever attain to say: 'My expectation is from God'? (Psalm 62:5). Being, for Bible and Qur'an, already there in creation, its further index would need to relate to all ensuing there. Tribe and place-tenure being such elemental aspects of our humanity, it would be natural for anticipations of divine relation to find occasion there. Such was precisely the founding Biblical tradition. Divine action would centre round 'our' story and be evident in 'our' affairs. Faith would be 'race-and-people' centred, as if to play into the hands of latter-day sceptics, reading religion as vested interest in a private transcendence.

Things corporate and social being basic to humankind, 'expectation' as to meaning might well start there. A 'God with us' assurance would be fortifying for any people, seeking to territorialise their identity and travelling meanwhile through lands that threatened their transit thither. The Biblical scenario plainly belongs there. Yahweh was 'forthcoming' in terms urgent and basic to human factuality, had in ancestry and land security, people knowing themselves by the sanction of their story.

Its burden, however, was that it was competitive. Tribe was possessedly unique but perennially diverse. It would be long and far before conviction, coming this way, would arrive to sing:

All people that on earth do dwell
Sing to the Lord with cheerful voice,
Him serve with fear, His praise forthtell.
Come ye before Him and rejoice.

That resounding 'Old Hundredth' psalm and hymn could only come by way of the intimate 'we Thy people' scheme of answered expectation which gave it birth. Expectations might revise themselves as evidenced in the rise of Christianity.

But 'forthcoming-ness', answering to human sense awaiting it and the scenes where selfhood moved, might be looked for more in terms of law and education, than of tribe and tribal story. If we argued from tenancy and tenure, rather than who enjoyed these, then 'guidance' directing our behaving and 'régime' ordering our society would seem supremely requisite and, therefore, divinely 'expectable' from that beyond.

Such conjecture was realised in Islam though – *ex hypothesi* – in no way devised by it, Islam being the most confidently 'clue-given' of all religions. The human situation is seen as satisfactorily monitored, equipped and disciplined by law, ordinance, structure and power. Allah fulfilled all due expectancy, dispelling all disabling 'ignorance' and making plain and feasible 'the straight path' wherein to walk. There has been full discharge of divine 'duty' towards us (as Surah 4.165 insists) in thus enabling a muslim humankind.

Like the tribally realised requisite, it has its logic in that the situation it addresses truly has that need. Lawlessness would ruin all. A responsible Creator and 'Inviter' into 'dominion' would surely need to be a lawgiver or be gravely in default. We are, of course, free to argue that all necessary law could be devised by our own resources of reason, case-making about 'common good', or the 'greatest happiness principle' or careful study of psychic patterns and their wise treatment. So doing, however, would take us out of all perception of transcendence with which we began and bring the disputanda back to the open verdict about ourselves that has to be resolved by ourselves.

Back to Islam. Does the very necessity of law contain its fallibility as any final solution to the human tangle? Without it our frailty would be in worse case. It witnesses to the dignity of a destiny to good and truth and wisdom, yet it also registers – if it does not provoke – our perversity. What it requires of justice, honesty and well-being, it does not of itself ensure. It leaves uncorrected the capacity we have to defy it. When that happens it can only condemn and requite. These may only sometimes avail to redeem the situation they concern. The many other times, wrong wins in that it abides, whether in resentment, or deeper wickedness. There are inward guilts law has no skill to identify, still less amend. Where it succeeds in law-abiding it may kindle unworthy elements of pride or snob-bery or censure. It seems to point to requisites beyond its own competence in the very urgency of its validity, while conscience always needs to reckon with the contents in law's writ.

Hence what Christianity learned to seek – and believed to find – from the same forthcoming transcendence the other theisms also trusted to respond, namely an enterprise of redeeming grace, pondered in preceding chapters. At least it widened, into some measure of inclusive humanity, that 'we-Thy-people' theme to which it owed so much and paid such grateful tribute. Then the splendid 'Old Hundredth' could be sung and felt without compromise or contradiction, in the Christ who had dismissed the crowding merchants from 'the court of the Gentiles' where the Temple 'barred' them.

This Christian perception of 'the grace of God' forthcoming from, and as, the divine mind in the human direction as 'the Word made flesh' in 'time's sacrament' through Cross and Passion, kept faith in its different way with the Islamic yearning for a divine law to guide our human will. It had for this what it called 'the law of Christ', 'ruling hearts and minds'. Until it became 'Christendom' it had abjured the thought of a powered religion, of a law that had sanctions of system and order other than conscience and grace. Since that Constantinian change it has struggled to obey again the priority of its first origin via the New Testament. The contemporary world is more and more requiring that it win the struggle. For these disputanda we are discussing are partly inside all faiths as well as being between them and all at any distance from them.

The 'Christendom' issue apart, Christianity has deep domestic 'fissures' to which thought must now turn and defer till later what may be incom-plete thus far in the more philosophical aspects of a right theology. What of Christology – always the working heart, if not the Achilles' heel, of Christian theology? The New Testament is the critical arena of its pros and cons. The whole case here is – and must remain – that 'the faith was in the finding' just as love is in exchange with love, not as an easy bargain but as a right affinity. Could Jesus *not* have been of the identity and quality to bring to pass the faith that so reported him? Could that faith have cred-ibly come to birth had he been otherwise? Did faith find him, and find itself, only by a sorry delusion either way?

'No they could not' has been the answer here throughout. It is only honest if it faces the proffered answers to the contrary. Yes, the faith was a distortion of the real Jesus. Yes, its birth was otherwise, in sad misreading or even wilful falsifying of its alleged evidences.

There is irony either way, in that the New Testament will be the major quarry from which evidences are drawn, confidently by those who trust its witness, ambiguously by those who do not, as citing an authority to which so much of what they disavow is nevertheless uniquely owed. For little would be known of any 'Jesus of history' had there never been 'the Christ of faith' bequeathing the texts to tell him. This central role of the New Testament document itself in all disputanda means that it is both the arbiter and the arbitrated in the issues over which it presides.

It is true that, from archaeology and research, there is more ample knowledge than there used to be of 1st century Judaism and, for example, of the culture of Galilee in Jesus' day, than was earlier available – much of it from assiduous Jewish scholarship occupied with the Dead Sea Scrolls. There is always, for scholarship, on every side, the lurking animus of what a *parti pris* would wish to be the case. With such we have mutually to cope and honestly to contend. A wholly understandable Jewish emotion about a purloined Jewish Jesus needs a ready Christian relation that does not harden the issue by dint of emotive counter-theses. Meanwhile, the task of objective study is to maximise all that can be known, of Rome and Greece and Jewry and Palestine, during the decisive birth-years of Christianity.

What questions can be duly answered always depends on how they are phrased. Did Jesus intend the Church is one whose phrasing makes it inadmissible, since the emerging concept of a 'church' derived only from his legacy. But, like many legacies, it was not had except in the form that being legatee received it. *Ab initio*, there were certainly disciples who came to perceive themselves as having a role like Moses' elders. That role, ripened into apostolate, was readily acknowledged in the emerging community as crucial to its fellowship. Paul, the untimely addition, earnestly coveted the right to share it.

That 'Messiah' might have a collective meaning, however singular the event 'he' must be, was present in the tradition, as plainly discerned from any 'chosen people' of whom and to whom and through whom 'Messiah' alone could be, or come, or save. With the ever-present proviso of 'trusting the text', Jesus had spoken of the future, seen it as long lasting and linked with 'those who had been with him'. It proved so solicitously the cherisher of his sayings in Gospels we can never dispense with, and scantily replenish, in knowledge of his teachings. Hindsight may see how implicitly he 'intended the Church' in the service it uniquely rendered him – unless we assume that he was indifferent to the fate of his words, and so, in turn, disinterested in their meaning.

Is there not also an implied 'intention for a church' (if not for what ensued as the Church) in the reading of his Passion he himself enshrined in Holy Communion? Beyond – but in no way despite – those 'teachings', he would be remembered, as we saw earlier, in 'the breaking of the bread'.

That future ritual, as it came to be, focused on the significance of how and why he died and sealed that significance in communal meal. It was odd, therefore, for Adolf Harnack, 19th century historian, to say: 'Jesus preached the kingdom of God and what happened was the Church' and mean it as a gibe. 'The kingdom of God' he had told them is 'in your midst', i.e. 'among you communally' (Luke 17:21) – the translation 'within you' is much misconstrued, as if denoting some private piety or mystic sense. (The word is plural.) 'There am I in the midst' was a familiar assurance. Neither the story nor the teaching of Jesus suggest a continuity of private devotees. Nor, even by definition, could 'teaching' exclude some *magisterium* beyond its time, into its future, though what its perpetuation could not lack it would need itself to control.

But if 'intention for church' could be credibly detected in many aspects of Jesus' ministry and of his Passion, what of the situation the other way round, of a 'church intention' with Jesus? Here there are so many conjectures to perplex. This perception of 'divine descent' – was it not wholly owed to 'Gentile', even pagan, factors likening the risen Jesus to an 'emperor deified'? Deifications were familiar strategy of Roman power as a means of 'rewarding' prowess in the field and of reducing the masses to awed subjugation by a 'myth' no intelligent parties believed. Were not 'Gentiles' anyway taking over the Church, reshaping any Jesus' legacy in their own image?

The notion holds no water. The direction was all the other way. 'Incarnation' was never told, read or meant as 'deification'. The second was wholly inconceivable in the Jewish matrix where all things Christian had their anchorage. To that cradle of mind the New Testament writers were ever loyal, citing its precedents, arguing – like the Letter to the Hebrews – from its rituals and claiming a single heritage. Themes about divine rendezvous were as old as Jacob's 'ladder', while 'I am come down to deliver' was as old as the Exodus.

As noted earlier, this sense of divine 'agency' with divine ends was perennial in the whole prophetic tradition. 'Messengers' were duly sent, as in Jesus' own parable, to a human vineyard where tenants were accountable and, on every score, required to be 'visited' if their destiny and Yahweh's sovereignty together were not to be forfeit. When that sent prophethood theme ripened into Messianic hope of still more inclusive 'intervention', there was every Judaic reason for discerning it in the human in which alone it could transpire. 'I will send to them my Son' had a thoroughly Biblical ring, seeing that 'servant' and 'son' were near synonymous.

So much we have seen. The point now is to let the logic tell against the notion of some subversion of Jewish norms of thought on Yahweh by aberrations due to Graeco-Roman influences. Doubtless, when the faith spread into their physical territory it responded to their milieu. That is not in doubt. The Johannine *logos*, allied to the Hebrew *dabar*, is evident enough, serving that Gospel's linking of incarnate language to the *fiat* of creation, with Paul earlier doing the same concerning 'the God who shined . . .' – than which there could be no clearer Jewish figure of speech.

Was Paul, in this context, the arch mischief-maker? So many have opined. Paul, Harnack alleged, had 'wrecked the religion of Jesus on the Cross of Christ,' which was to ignore or deny two fundamental things, namely how only in sequence to that Cross had his 'religion' been preserved in written accessibility to have us know, in any wealth of data, what that 'religion' had been, and, secondly, how the Cross had eventuated from human attitudes to the teaching his 'religion' brought. For its 'prosperity' as teaching, in a world hostile to its genius, came only in and through the Passion.

To cast Paul as a 'renegade' and the New Testament with him as some Jewish 'treason' is quite to discount the deep tension of the Jew/Christian situation which he underwent in his own spirit and suffered in his own career. No 'traitor' could have agonised so intensely over the 'development' he had been moved to serve. For the travail went very deep. It was hard indeed for a deeply loyal Jew to concede that the time had come to accept faith-community with 'Gentiles' as the proper destiny of the Judaic world, and to identify that sense of radical obedience as made evident by so incongruous a drama as a crucified sufferer. It was not only a matter of privilege loathe to let itself be shared: it was to allow it so at whatever personal cost.

Despite Harnack's verdict there was much in common between the 'Jewishness' of Jesus and factors in Paul's Damascus road conversion. It was no chance that he 'heard' the voice say: 'I am Jesus.' The 'persecution' was of the Jesus Saul saw as misguided precisely in its being directed on to the Church. For by Saul's prescripts there was an intimate connection between his zeal and the antipathy felt for Jesus by Saul-like critics during the months of ministry leading to the Cross as its culmination.

The issue, as we saw in the chapter on 'Our Lord Jesus Christ', was not initially between Jew and Christian but between versions of Jewishness that Jesus himself broached and which the life of the Church extended into 'Gentile' inclusion. Inside the latter, reproach of Paul as 'treasonous' would have to be taken within that now contrasting sense of the term 'Jewish', namely 'Jews' creating an embracing church, and 'Jews' reading themselves categorically loyal in decrying it.

The always ardent efforts Paul made to demonstrate his abiding Jewishness, in writing to Galatians and others, argue that to find him false to Jewry is to deny there was ever any issue, in the very legacy of Jesus and the life of the Church, about the self-understanding of Jewry. Or it is to think that for several decades it was not an open question. It would also be to ignore the pain, for both parties, which living through it entailed.

All that was there at stake takes the course of thought back to the Cross itself, with the place it has in Christianity alleged to be a gross exaggeration of, or a misguided version about, the actual event. There are, it is true, several vital points of detail about the trial or trials of Jesus, the legalities and niceties of Sanhedrin process and the inter-action of Jewish and Roman stakes. There are also deep, and perhaps impenetrable, questions about the inner consciousness of Jesus.

What of the first and second, for they inter-depend? Disputing wants to say that too much, in Passion theology, is made to hinge on too little. Christian imagination – no more – has come to be fixated on 'the wondrous Cross', unable to reckon with its de-glamourised reality. A sad, a heinous, miscarriage of justice, in unhappy coincidences of time and place, has been made to 'take away the sin of the world' and to belong to 'One slain before the foundation of the world'. This devout hyperbole – no less – has to be clipped into perspective.

'Justice in miscarriage' all would agree. The Beatitudes ought not to be fated to a preacher's Gethsemane. Indeed not, but still the two belong in one story. Jesus' crucifixion, indeed, has all the marks of 'miscarriage' with more than 'justice' darkly in forfeit. Even so, minimal assessments of liability would still have to recognise a true mirroring of the world, its culpable politics, its dangerous prides, its conspiratorial perversity. 'Sin of the world' was not a formula to do other than find the 'blame' human-wide. What critics call 'exaggeration' had better be 'characterisation' where that *'ecce homo'* of Pilate becomes *'Ecce homines'* – 'the likeness of our sinfulness', placarding without palliative the human world.

That at least was how it seemed to be – and to have been – in the retrospect that shaped the Church. Suffering for their fidelity had long been the pattern familiar to prophethood and often rehearsed in scripture and in parable, and by Jesus himself. If human wrong were ever to find one focal, real symbol it could be here, whatever the 'accidents' that might have to be included in the story. The drama itself was no 'mishap'. All else would turn – and that centrality itself – on how the lonely sufferer belonged in the event.

Reported 'darkness over the land' did not prevent the sheer visibility of the Passion. There has been conjecture in some quarters asking: What if Jesus had been walled up to die of hunger, forever out of sight, or left like some Joseph down a forgotten well? To be crucified was to be public property. Reportedly, it happened so. What of the words from the Cross? How were they known for abiding inner disclosure of their meaning? Much that is vital is vulnerable to query – a situation that is no necessary veto on faith – a point which must recur in conclusion.

In earlier musings about divine 'forthcoming-ness', it was suggested that 'guidance' dispelling ignorance and 'system' managing waywardness would not suffice the human situation. The ultimate 'sufficing' might then be found where Christian faith thought to identify it, namely redemption in 'Christ and him crucified'. This is not to say that any faith is authentic merely because it came about and took itself for authentic. It is to say that such an outcome requires due reckoning with its origin.

That point brings us to that third dimension of sceptical critique, namely the inner consciousness of Jesus. We earlier studied the antecedents of the Cross – always with that proviso about 'trusting the narratives'. They see him discerning, in the gathering logic of his ministry, 'the cup his Father gives', after the pattern of 'the suffering servant' and in the meaning of 'Messiah'.

That consensus of the Gospels is hotly rejected by the contrasted view that sees in Jesus a charismatic, a wandering preacher of a type readily detectable by Jewish scholarship in the society of 1st century Jewry. This 'disputing' of any Christian Jesus is a vigorous part of his alleged rescue from an interpretation that, in the interests of its own dogma, has quite violated the reality – a reality open to access for those who will allow the evidence about 'Jesus the Jew'.

The Jewishness of Jesus has never sanely been in doubt. The question has always been 'Jewish in what terms?' That open question, as we have seen with Paul, was in the very fabric of Christian making as, initially, a wholly Jewish thing. Jesus, long before 'Christians annexed' him, had been radically at issue with other Jews about the law, the Sabbath, the generous love of Yahweh and the right of conscience over against rabbinic authority and the handling of texts.

Even so, it is insisted, we should understand that Jesus was 'a Jewish holy man, a preacher and an exorcist', armed with moral aphorisms and heralding the imminent arrival of the kingdom of God. Dr. Geza Vermes of Oxford, erudite veteran of Hebrew studies, sees a Jesus closely akin to another of the same type, a certain Hanina Ben Dosa, his Galilean contemporary and one of many such. Any Christian reservation about such a parallel should not exclude the possibility or be dismissive of its documentation. 'The Word made flesh' means that Incarnation is identified by time and place and the immediacies it must share – as we saw in Chapter Two – if it be 'in time' at all. What, however, it is fair to ask is why we find no cathedrals in many a capital city of the world, no churches dotted across landscapes, consecrated in the name of Hanina Ben Dosa.

That worldwideness may, indeed, be fortuitous, the strange, unaccountable fortune, or misfortune, as a history that should never have been. It is no part of faith to ask for guarantee of its content or to hold that something only has to happen to be authentic. Truth does not invite us into certitude: it summons us into trust. Trust of that order will find some reassurance in the worldwideness of Christian conviction about Jesus as the Christ, as being a phenomenon no Hanina Ben Dosa would ever either engender or explain.

It is noteworthy that Dr. Vermes was able to posit this near identity between Jesus and Hanina Ben Dosa – though noting that Jesus was incomparably superior – by excluding altogether from his Jesus the Messianic dimension, this – for him despite all evidence to the contrary – being the misreading into which the New Testament had been beguiled. That scholarly register of something 'incomparable' of course drew that part of its conclusion from the Gospels it otherwise has to suspect.

At all events, it is by that Messianic theme Christianity stands and by it, as the very name demands, is identified. Within the story of Jesus it gives coherence to all else. It is deep in the Lord's Prayer itself – those pleas about 'kingdom', 'will', and 'hallowing of the Name', and (if, as well we may, we read it so) 'Give us this day Messiah's bread'. It belongs with all the 'servant' precedents to which Jesus referred and which he notably associated with the Jerusalem ('Thou that killest . . .') whither 'he must go'. It lives in the emphasis on 'this Passover' celebrated there with such presaging of the tragic climax near at hand.

The Jewish urge to have a Jesus in the Hanina Ben Dosa image chimes with a rejection of 'the stranger from heaven' theme it reads and rejects in the Johannine Christ as a 'heavenly traveller in temporary exile on earth who is longing to return to his real home'. Jewish realism deplores that story of Jesus 'as a momentary phase in the external existence of the Son'. Have not 'Gentile' categories taken over, in travesty, the Judaic prerogative of a people-centred theism?

'Temporary exile' from heaven was never the evangelists' perception of heaven's loving compassion, in a most Hebraic way, stooping to the human condition. The 'temporary' was never description of the 'temporal' in the meaning of incarnation. 'Time' there had to be, as where humans are, but the sojourn had its 'temporal' character as being the forthcomingness of the Eternal. Hosea would at once have understood, for his Yahweh, he thought, had cried: 'O my people, how shall I give you up?' (11:8). It was entirely that for which Job had yearned in anguish: 'O that I knew where I might find him!' (23:3). Would not Messianic achievement be where the answer was – in utterly Jewish terms – as where in history He would truly be and be truly? We seem to be forced back to the conclusion that what is at issue between a Messianic and a non-Messianic Jesus is not, at the outset, an issue dividing Jew from Christian, but one dividing Jew from Jew.

If so, though distinctively 'Gentile' factors filtered into Christianity in keeping with its open reach, but without essentially altering its Jewish nativity, there should be no animus either way. 'Gentile' Christians are 'Jewish' in terms that founding Christian Jews had believed genuinely loyal. Tragically, however, much animus remains and remains to be dispelled by will to love. A gathering disavowal of those founding souls, not least after the Fall of Jerusalem with its dire imperilling of Jewish tradition, coincided with the growing 'Gentile' adhesion to the Church.

Antipathies then hardened into enmity and calumny, all too tragically obscuring and defacing the history. The Prologue of John had read the story in its essence from afar, in that it was 'his own' that – at length 'received him not'. There would be wonder and pain that an impossible paradox had happened. The mothering world had proved blind: its legitimate offspring would become rejectionist.

The disputanda of the centuries made Jewry's 'world harsh and strange' as ethnicized and politicized into bitterness and persecution and a Christendom betrayed its Christianity in radical disowning of its debts and criminal pursuing of its malice. The tasks of theology around 'the Christian Jesus' are still desperately hindered by the wrongs, the memory of wrongs, the guilt of wrongs, which still besiege it. It often seems unforgivably academic to stay – as here – with the intellectual issues, and would in truth be so were the others not earnestly and ever in mind.

But what, in all liability for 'the Christian Jesus' and the themes of Christology, are we really seeking? Why should it matter? Does the world care? Is theology, with or without Christology, anything that longer matters? All questions apart as to whether Jesus was 'the Christianity-destined one' or whether he was his own Hanina Ben Dosa, what the ado anyway? Why not let such sleep-inducing business merely slumber? Should not Christian theology take hint out of Leonardo Da Vinci's *Notebook* where he wrote: 'O Leonardo, why toilest thou so?'

Why indeed? It was only a moment of weariness. He still pursued his vocation with unresting intellectual piety of mind. For he could do no other. Between that ever questing will to understand and an external world of things, laws and forces, there was a bonding affinity. There were 'wombs of stone' from which to conjure 'children unto God'. There were scenes and faces which his paints and brushes would bequeath to waiting generations. Everywhere shapes awaited etchings and observation could

[109]

yield devices for inventiveness. Men might even fly if only they could contrive (as well they might) wings like birds and overcome the gravity that held them to the ground.

On every hand there was a world meant for his human wit and will and these, in his attentive, self-expending energies, were fitted to that world. It would be gross dis-courtesy, if not intellectual treason, to fail to ask what lay on the other side of this so generously inviting thing human experience was found to be. Neither he nor the guest-making earth explained their own existence, still less did they explain the endless surprise discovered in their fusion. Theism is no more, no less, than a wide-awake-ness in the very core of life, a sense of something reciprocal without which I would not be the me I am, nor my world the thing it is.

Leonardo Da Vinci's religious faith was not shouted from the roof-tops, it was confessed in his activities and in his notes and sketches. The Church of his day had too many compromises and moral embarrassments to satisfy the critical mind. There was something 'protestant' about his cast of soul. 'What do you think, Man, of your own species?' was the basic question. Our senses are of and from the earth, but the reason they furnish within us passes into contemplation. Spiritual truths were legible everywhere in the fabric of these things, as when he observed: 'An arch is nothing less than the strength caused by two weaknesses.' 'Whom do I see?' he asked of the sculptor's world: 'I see the Saviour crucified anew' was the reply.

This genius from the late Middle Ages, then, would have all our disputanda around 'God in Christ' come round at length to the clue in 'our own species' and refuse the despondency or the truancy that will not read our liability to privilege and distrusts the invitation into the society of the God in whom we could discern its source, its waiting grace.

What, though, distrusting that serenity of confident faith, the truants will say, about our legitimate despair? For is there an honesty that will not languish and mourn at the spectacle of history? 'Let the street be as wide,' Leonardo wrote, 'as the universal height of the houses.' It is not so in the squalors of the centuries, the wrongs and crimes that deny a spacious living to multitudes of the oppressed, the poor, the despised. Faith in the divine grace that willed – it could otherwise be said – is surely thwarted, if not cancelled by another sort of clue in 'our own species', which is its hand dyed in 'the sin of the world'.

An optimistic theism is a contradiction in terms. 'God in Christ' is not such. It holds in one the good creation and the crucial redemption. Crucial is the right word. For it has, in both realms, the nature of the Cross. 'The Lamb', as the seer in Patmos learned, was 'slain before the foundation of the world'. The vocation into hospitality of a divine order which Da Vinci has helped us to realise, was by its nature fraught with the risk of the truancy from it which we humans, in pride and perversity, would choose. We could not actively trust that 'good creation – as we must in order rightly to possess it – without the good redemption, a redemption good both in its retrieval of the primal hope and its healing of our wounds. How cryptically did our Leonardo understand divine redemption as the truth of his world of human arts when he wrote:

> In all parts of Europe there shall be lamentations by great nations for the death of one man who died in the East.

Faith in that 'Christian Jesus', as always and ever the measure of a faith in God, validates for us the legitimacy, indeed the privilege, of the scientific world but requires acceding gladly to the authority of the redemptive love, and of the Cross as that love's crowning symbol by which to teach us worship and compassion.

Another sort of dispute looms. 'Nativity' and 'Passion' – are these 'myths of God Incarnate', we should be 'adult' enough to forego, if not rather to despise? That 'myth' word needs more rigorous, less ready, usage. It conceals big mischief if usage fails to distinguish between what is fantasy and make-belief and what is authentic in a necessary shape, between 'telling tall tale' and a 'telling that is truly told'. How is anything truly 'told', if not – when of that order – in 'blood, sweat and tears'? Things have often told themselves in inclusive gesture and have recruited means because means were in the meaning. Thus they became party to the relevance.

'Mother' being instrumental to birth, Mary as mother is indispensable to Jesus born. A Jesus born is the *sina qua non* of 'God in Christ'. His birth, then, is in intention present in the being of the God who is (essentially and 'is to be' time-wise for our sakes) 'God in Christ'. That truth – if truth it is to be – implies a 'birth' which is both God's and that of Jesus in 'becoming' 'God's Christ'. 'Virginal nativity', then, could have point in this double perspective birth has, in that understanding of the event it is. Given the ground-faith in divine action (without which there is no such event), there is no 'magic' about 'imaginary forces'. Physical explory, if we wanted to pursue it, is not possible anyway and would be irrelevant even if it were. Mary's 'highly favoured-ness' belongs with 'God in Christ' – has, and asks, no other context.

'God in Christ' – again basically there in all dispute of faith with creed – being sacrament in time (in the sense studied in Chapters Two and Four) as divine, redeeming 'visitation', needs and argues a 'departure', in the wake of death, a death certified as such in 'burial'. Such 'departure' must then be through a tomb and into 'glory had before the world was'. 'God in Christ', then, contains for theology precisely an empty tomb, known as such only in that inherent sequence of a redeemng economy that belongs with God. Again, as with Mary, the physical 'verification' – if we wanted it – is in the very nature of the case inaccessible. Nor would the meaning be any more secure if it were ever feasible, as detectives might, to 'establish' its 'emptiness'. Nor would 'God in Christ' this way (death and resurrection) be any less as faith knows them, if sifting through all arguable scenarios ever demonstrated a rightly identified, untenanted, 1st century grave. Nor does faith want or need vindication by such investigative success or non-success.

Thus what is popularly dubbed 'myth' is not 'myth' at all unless transcendence with will to create and redeem is also 'myth'. So to think, of course, would have us disqualifying the truth of 'our own species', and so dissolving into futility what occupied our disputanda.

There is much nonsense also in the usage of the term 'supernatural', so often to the fore in allegations of 'myth' and the 'mythical'. 'Super', anyway is cripplingly ambiguous – not least so when tied on to 'natural', as if the two were disparate: or to imply that there was nothing between 'the law of the evidence of the test-tube' and 'the waving of the magic wand'.

What of an orchestra rendering those glorious, gathering strains of Beethoven's Ninth Symphony' and its 'Hymn to Joy?' Guts – of cats maybe – strings, winds in shapes, noises, timings, seconds, booms, taps, vocal chords, a medley of 'natural causes' happening in their physical incidence, their native force and quality. But, hark! all that quantity in its natural, physical, indispensable condition becoming the medium of emotion, in a summoning of hope and wonder, in a telling of the otherwise untold, a physical poem, a natural performance that had not 'left a gap in nature' but had nature filling it with near celestial music.

Faith's sacrament in 'the Christian Jesus' is something of this order and this mystery. For, in their strict sense both words convey this unison between time and meaning, between what indwells what it transcends and transcends where it indwells, while it thoroughly belongs with both. Incarnation is not about the divine erupting into where it may not belong, nor the human perverting or usurping what it has no power to tell. As, even in the lowly realm of verbal metaphor, there is a fusion where neither is unseemly in the borrowing and neither dishonoured in the exchange. God may be known appropriately to the divine nature in the Christ whom that nature owns and, in that same enterprise of grace, endow the human with the dignity and the significance of such employ. How well the Incarnation fits a world in which the ordinary is the most extra-ordinary thing of all.

Disputers may feel they have one final demur before the act of faith. Why, it may be asked, is this way of divine grace and patience not more effective – the pragmatists will say efficient – in the world? Christianity has no monopoly of genuine saints, no dearth of real sinners. It might be, as George Eliot thought in her agnostic years,

> The highest expression of the religious sentiment that has yet found its place in the history of mankind.

Why, then, is it so far unfulfilling of its promise? It will not do to say that, even if as failure, alongside religions of law, or special covenant, or cosmic ambivalence, it is a worthier failure. The burden of its unwantedness lies essentially in its ever uncompulsive quality. 'To stand at the door and knock' was the Christ way from the last book in the Bible and from the onset of his ministry. A compulsive salvation, a coercing grace, would be a contradiction of the terms. Moreover, coercion had never been the divine mode, seeing that the understanding of creation told a divine 'let there be' and saw this applying to our human 'dominion'. To have made coercive any strategy of grace would have taken it out of 'the real world'. We would need to argue that it would have been better to have humans helpless automata from the beginning. But then that is not how we are. Worthy failure may be all that grace can look for in those quarters that will it shall be such.

We are left to a final conclusion. It is that Christian faith consists in a will to faith, a will kindled by the truth that waits for it. This has been our case throughout. Trust in Christ, in the Christ-likeness of God, is a venture, not a theory nor a gamble. There has to be a courage to believe, a courage that tests and stays ready to be tested. There has to be what elsewhere Donne called an 'inter-assurance of the minds' – the mind that trusts and the mind-for-us in 'God in Christ', either establishing the other.

'I am a sort of illicit Christian,' wrote Edwin Muir, whom we met in Chapter One, 'I have faith but I cannot belong to any one Christian community.' Of such, potentially, is 'the kingdom of heaven'. Meanwhile some ready for the larger risk of creed and community, of 'bread and wine' after 'the water of baptism' may continue, by that order of fidelity, to sustain the necessary fabric whereby 'faith does not perish from the earth'. So – as perhaps otherwise it might not be – 'whoso-ever will may come'.

It is time to turn, in a concluding chapter, to the experience of 'love's exchange' – the Christ of Christians and the Christians with Christ.

CHAPTER SEVEN

Love's Exchange

The near extinction of the personal pronouns singular 'thee' and 'thou' in modern English usage has sadly diminished the expressiveness of life and love in our society. The common 'each and all' in plural 'you' disable the warmth, fervour and intensity that can pour into the feel of 'thou'. Biblical psalmody and Christian hymnody are still more deeply impoverished by the change, with the Authorised Bible and William Shakespeare in their company. 'What can you do for me?' is a poor alternative to 'Canst thou not minister to a mind diseased' and something in the disparity comes through the meaning wanting and suiting the pronoun it prefers.

The point in this concluding chapter about 'the Christian Jesus' is not that we cannot mean sincerely unless our diction is archaic. It is that there is something about being Christian which clings to all the 'thou' word used to hold in its relation to its Lord. Hence its unfailing appearance in translation of Greek and Latin hymns and in the songs Charles Wesley gave to Methodism. These can readily slip into the third person – as indeed they must in loyalty to an historic faith. 'My song is love unknown' stays there throughout: 'What has my Lord done?' 'My Lord should take frail flesh and die', and 'For his death they thirst and cry', as events urging the reply his 'I' must bring. 'Has He marks to lead me to Him?' asks Stephen of Mar Saba, to condition his question: 'If He be my guide.' Yet everywhere this 'me' and this 'third party' pass into the intimacy only 'Thou' can fit and tell.

So we find the faith singing perennially 'Thou joy of loving hearts', 'Thou fount of life', 'Thou light of men . . .' 'Thou sweetness most ineffable in whom all joys are found . . .' 'O love that will not let me go, I rest my weary soul in Thee'. Moods or minds noted in the previous chapter would cite all this as proof of their own thesis about wilful illusion, or perhaps only of their own distance from its reasons. Yet it remains elemental in how we have a 'Christian Jesus', namely as loved and lover in the immediacy of 'Thou' and 'I'. It has to be a personal devotion in order that it may be a public discipleship, so that the emotion is not religiously indulgent nor the discipleship routine or perfunctory. Faith, as we have seen, has its academic obligations but betrays itself if it is merely a satisfaction in the mind. Where love belongs, satisfactions are never in the mind alone.

Even so, the exchange of love between Christian and Christ does well to begin there, if it is to be duly alert and aware of the world. It will then have more truly its other characteristics as expressive and expending. The three – intellectual, expressive and expending – will best denote this chapter's task in exposition.

It has been decisive throughout that Christianity stands in, and stands by, truth as given and as received and only these in their inter-action. There was the Christ for faith's cognisance and faith's cognisance found him the Christ he was. Its cognition answered his identity as present to evoke it. We have wanted and needed to ask who Jesus must have been to have had the sequel which was apostolic faith and, conversely, how that faith could have otherwise resulted without the Jesus it reported.

Living as it does with disputanda earlier reviewed, faith is plainly intellectually liable about the love it tells. It stands squarely in and for 'the intellectual love of God', a love that can be 'lost in wonder and praise' but not as if to 'heights of fancy'. It is love which bids it be 'trinitarian' in that the Holy Spirit 'takes the things of Christ' in an exegesis to us. Those 'things of Christ' – as he could say – were, by the whole meaning of 'time's sacrament', the very things of God.

In this 'intellectual love', by which we answer Christ's, theology – we might say – becomes companionable. We realise it pursues a strategy which is lovable alike in content and in form. There is 'humanity' in its coming to us, as the very way of incarnation. 'Companionable', from its Latin source as 'taking bread with . . .', befits divinity seeking us in our own realm, our own idiom, becoming comprehensible inside conditions of our comprehension. When Plato, in his Greek intellectualism, could think it 'an odd thing for a man to say he loved a god', 'God in Christ' would resolve all such misgivings. The surest education happens best in accepting the point from which it should be starting.

To be sure, his 'coming in to tarry with us' has to be understood as one with 'Our God is a consuming fire' as Hebrews 12:29 insists, nor does the Incarnation annul. To discern in 'the Christian Jesus' a lovable strategy is, with him, to have the eternal Father in Whom all belongs and derives. Only so can incarnation inform our theology.

The point is important in that 'love to the Christian Jesus' *might* seem to dispense with the inclusive reality of God. In some forms of piety it can almost be that this has happened. If so, the corrective is in understanding more wisely and reckoning well with the ambiguity we concede in the double use of the word 'Lord'. It is intriguing to realise how it was just there that credal Christology began to find shape. 'Lord Jesus Christ' enlisted the same word as had told of 'The Lord God almighty'. *Te Deum Laudamus* came to open with 'We acknowledge Thee to be the Lord' in sequence to 'Thee, being God, we praise'. When 'Lord' recurs five times in the concluding suffrages, it embraces 'Father' and 'Son' in one 'ever-lastingness'.

'Lord', in that inclusive way, can duly tell the whole 'sign' of Incarnation, God's being in action, God's action in being, in their single character and purpose. But we must love aright 'with all our mind'. There has been a danger, in love less right, almost to have Jesus in the place of God. It sometimes seemed that way with a passionate thinker like Blaise Pascal, despite his fervour about 'the God of Abraham'. Somehow, in the end, his theology would cleave to Jesus as to none else. Feodor Dostoevsky, likewise, was bold at times to say that if there had to be choice he would opt for Christ rather than for God. His proper point was taken in Chapter Six, namely that a Christless God, a mere spectator God, a tyrant throned, he would have to reject – and reject for profoundly theological reasons which 'a Christ' alone satisfied. Otherwise, he argued that atheism would be his only option.

Just as there has been misguided Jesus-ology, missing the entire reality of 'God in Christ' duly told in Christology, so there have also been intolerable theologies of arbitrary despotism or absolute fickleness that only something like a Christ could duly banish. The Christ-likeness of God alone underwrites the theology worthy of God – which is another way of saying that 'the Father sent the Son', making these for ever 'this Father and this Son', where a fully intellectual theology is happy to arrive and blessed in the arriving.

It is useful in this context to pause at the striking words 'very God of very God' in the Nicene Creed – so hard to render right in many languages. For the thought is finely wrought. 'Very' is only applied to nouns in English for occasions of heavy emphasis, as in 'Those were his very words', or 'That was the very moment when . . .' Otherwise 'very' sharpens other adjectives, as when 'we are very bitter'. It then simply intensifies a condition which is not in doubt, rather than implies interrogation of one that is.

So what is the point in its double use in the Creed and attaching to the noun 'God'? It has to do with a basic perplexity, if not puzzle, about 'incarnate God', the paradox we found the poets exploring in Chapter One. It might be alright for poets to muse about 'an eternal Word unable to speak of a word', but what of hard-headed theologians, Jewish ones most of all? How could they hold such incredible notions of 'the Lord

God throned above all heavens'? How could it be the same God? Or conversely, this child, this nursling, this frequenter of highways, this man on that Cross – how could these be the Creator, 'eternal, invisible, God only wise'? Two such incompatibles, only pagan triviality or obscene Jewish treason, could possibly conjoin. 'God only undone' would be the urgent verdict of a true worship, refusing to be beguiled into folly and shame.

Yet, Biblically, as we have seen, this 'bizarre' situation is not without analogy. 'Who has believed our report?' asks Isaiah 53:1, concerning where 'the arm of the Lord' is revealed. The same incredulity is present – about a 'suffering Messiah' – and for similar reasons. This 'reporting' is beyond all honest, loyal credence. It offends all we have ever thought about that sublime figure, 'the mighty redeemer of Israel'. Nevertheless, the truth was with it – the truth that only the future could come to understand. Meanwhile the prophet messenger held on to his 'absurdity' about how 'the pleasure of the Lord' would prosper in *his* hand, the Lord's and Messiah's.

Nor is the credence of the two incredibles unlinked. For what Isaiah calls 'report' is precisely what Pauline and Christian faith called 'tradition', in both cases 'that we have ourselves heard' being in turn 'that which we ourselves tell onward'. Isaiah's 'report' has this double sense of what is on our lips because it was in our ears. 'News' – to be such – is always heard and told, then told and heard. 'Very God of very God' – we might say – 'witnesses to witness' in a similar way. It reassures because doubt is reasonably present and faith should know how to anticipate the misgivings without which its whole content would be at risk, not because the doubts had no point but because they had no ground. Doubt is best satisfied by having its table turned – all of which is part of the intellectual love of God in the unloving world.

That the God of such love employs with us a lovable strategy by dint of 'the Word made flesh' can be perceived from another angle. One of the surest images of 'God in Christ' in the Biblical vocabulary is that of 'the face'. In 2 Corinthians 4:6, Paul tells his readers that 'We have the light of the knowledge of the glory of God in the face of Jesus Christ.' It is a typical Pauline sentence with its string of possessives. 'Light in the face' is a simple yet sublime analogy – a truth of poetic warrant. Paul links that light with the *Fiat Lux* that inaugurated creation.

His original, of course, is the Aaronic blessing laid down for Moses' brother in Numbers 6:23–27, where 'the light of the face of the Lord' lays His Name upon the people, in the meaning of priestly benediction and the pledge of 'His peace'. Used of 'the Christian Jesus', the face-imagery proves to be the surest index to the twin meanings of the Incarnation, the human for the divine, the divine through the human. For the face belongs to two realms. It is precariously physical – a congerie of muscle, skin, nerve, vein and sinew, all a marvel of physicality, splendidly beautiful, readily marred, a point of personality and the surest index to identity. All portraits need to include it: photography revels in its study.

Yet, in all those qualities of flesh and blood, that blanch and blush, that laugh and frown, it is a spiritual house, where wrinkles tell a history and a score of evident emotions move and have their being. Responses and reactions of the self behind disclose themselves in the physical movements by which it speaks. There could be no surer metaphor of things sacramental than the human face. It figures exactly what can be meant by a theology of 'Word made flesh', of the divine expressed within the human. 'The face of Christ' clearly means his whole significance as 'facial', not merely that item alone, however vital, but hand and foot and walk and heart in the unity of a historic scene through mortal years. The analogy abides in Paul reading this theme as 'treasure in earthen vessels' – all so susceptible, as the face is, to frailty and ridicule, if not calumny and wounds. Yet, even these in enmity may become factors in the light they yield to contemplation. 'A visage more marred than any' enters into the knowledge of God as there in the Passion of Jesus. What could it have meant for him there and then, when 'Jesus turned and looked on Peter'?

If it was the privilege of priestly Aarons to speak the divine 'light' of benediction, so it is the calling of the intellectual love of God to 'illumine' the world from the 'light of the face of Christ'. The 'earthen vessels' term Paul uses as being where, theologically, we have 'the light', 'mere pots of clay' *may* refer to the physical limitations he and other apostles were under – or even mishaps in their travel plans. For he was much battered in limb and faculty during those active years when he was writing. More probably, though, the 'vessels' are the thoughts, the words, the idioms, in which meanings are conveyed. Had he not drawn from Aaron the 'face' imagery for just that reason? To hand were many more, from precedents in Jesus' parables, or emulating what, elsewhere, would be Talmudic exegesis, or the insights of the Stoics.

Throughout, he made his case about Jesus in steady bearing on the vagaries as he found them in the churches. It was a love of 'God in Christ' won from the travail of his own earlier experience against the truth of it. He was always striving to overcome the debit of his 'late arrival' and he struggled with his theology from inside 'the care of all the churches', pressing on him daily. The vehemence in his spirit did not override the penetration of his mind, so that he was able to reach for early and definitive confessions of the faith, superlatively so in Philippians 2:5–11 about 'the mind of Christ' in that venture out of eternity into time, into birth, ministry, Passion and return through the gate of death into the same precedent eternity, now for ever known and knowable in the light of that story – as studied in Chapter Two. 'I am persuaded' (Romans 8:38 and 15:14) was a loved form of words for himself and 'commend', meaning 'let us establish together', what he preferred in 'reasonable' religion, so that truth might prosper by eliciting consent, as befitting its patience. 'Commend', in any event, was how God in Christ had the Gospel proceed (Romans 5:8).

In the once much loved medieval The Dream of the Rood, there came a part where the very tree of the Cross would speak of its role in the crucifixion. Only there, as blood-stained, nail-marked wood, had it place in the event, intimate yet measurelessly remote, when fragmented into numberless relics for the satisfying of local superstitions. Even so, for the New Testament mind, the intellectual love of God has found itself most moved to contemplation where that wood was made to stand.

Loving the Lord with all the mind has meant reckoning with how that Cross belongs with God. Paradox called to be searched where it most resided. Some parts of Christendom, it is true, tend to cohere around the Incarnation and humanity 'partaking of the divine nature' through its sacramental grace. 'The Son of God became the son of man, that the sons of men might become the sons of God.' But the Incarnation was ever inclusive of the Passion and would not, otherwise, have been truly in *our* world.

The human relevance of the Incarnation incorporates the human relevance of the Cross, from which we know that our sort of world is a crucifying place where love belongs only as venture into travail. The Cross as sign and measure of 'the sin of the world' belongs squarely with 'this Jesus' being 'the saviour of the world'. Writing, as we have believed we may, of 'the Christian Jesus' is to arrive at the love of God in its most luminous form. Hence what some have called 'Christ-mysticism' firmly in that Scripture. We 'love the Lord with all our mind' in accepting within ourselves his death as ours. It was not, as Shelley wrote:

A Promethean conqueror came:
Like a triumphal path, he trod
The thorns of death and shame.

Thorns were round the brow, not underfoot. There was nothing Promethean about Gethsemane. There was what Paul called a *kenosis*, a love including others at its own cost and for love's sake, in answer to their deepest need. 'This mind which was in Christ' had to be known as indicative of 'the mind of God'. For there had been such *kenosis* in the created order, in dignifying our creaturehood with an autonomy in trust with what was God's, risked into our liable tenant-custody. It would be divine *kenosis* still in the Holy Spirit partnering the Church through all its history bearing with 'broken vessels' and fractious folk.

Thus the love of God meant taking such *kenosis* into loving worship as ourselves partakers of its claim on personal life. Here were terms, identifiable by their own worth, in which one could know and love God, no longer in what was only majestical, holy, awesome and sublime concerning Him, but as – beyond and through these – infinitely worshipable from inside a world whose evidences, such Christian reading apart, told all too heavily against Him in all those other descriptives. The mind was liberated into the possibility of a theology that was honest about the human tragedy. The old prophet had spoken of 'the peace' of those whose minds 'stopped at God' (Isaiah 26:3) – 'stay' in the sense of 'concluding where one can rely', or 'relying so as to conclude' – in what seems a celebratory psalm about the securing of a city, or a reign, and perhaps playing on the Jerusalem word. The thought of 'staying on God this way' is fair summary of New Testament confidence. Its 'coming to rest' here in 'God in Christ' is not out of weariness over further pursuit, or fear further on to prove deceived, or resolving to be pragmatic. It springs from the deep satisfaction of where we have arrived, as to that which invites endless exploration of the open ends its consistency will hold.

Borrowing the prophet's language from its ancient context is in line with Paul's statement to his Corinthians (2:5:14) where he tells them: 'The love of Christ makes up our mind.' His Greek has the sense of 'brings us to decision', as when situations 'leave us no option', as blessedly 'hemmed in'. It makes up our mind about God, seeing that this 'God in Christ' expresses 'the Christ who is in God', where alone what the Incarnation had transpired to be was legible, and 'marvellous' in our eyes. So in turn, it makes up our mind about ourselves and the decisiveness leaves us no longer footloose and afraid. Or, in the language of the epistolary John: 'We know that the Son of God is come and has given us an understanding' (1:5:20).

In effect, we may say that 'the Christian Jesus' is our assurance that God is that sort of word. For what sort of word the word 'God' is has always been the problematic in using it. It somehow needs His own verifying as to what we should understand by having and using it. 'Jesus as the Word', in completion and confirmation of the entire significance of creation and our creaturehood as a right 'natural theology' has discerned these, would be just that verifying and the warrant for a worshipping theology in its terms. So much the Creeds surely meant in passing so readily from 'Maker of heaven and earth' to 'and in Jesus Christ, His only Son our Lord'.

Analogy of this perception of faith in Christ has often been drawn from art, poetry and literature. Here the art – in this credal sense – 'substantiates' the artist, the poem the poet, the writing the writer. Either party is fulfilled and known in the other. We can even merge them into one and say: 'I heard Beethoven', or 'I love Handel', or 'I study Shakespeare', where, in every case the one name covers the man and the work. It is something of this order (duly pondered as about eternal God) that happens when we find 'the Father and the Son' in the one referent 'God'. Such, in its subtle form – so oft misread – is the technical sense of the word 'begotten', just as the music of Mozart is Mozart in his music, and Shakespeare is both the drama and the dramatist.

That parallel, however, itself suggests how theological faith, or the intellectual love of God, has to be careful and vigilant. Literary criticism can be a highly charged discipline often at odds with itself, the works it handles being so variously appreciated. The vigilance of theology comes within the meaning of the Holy Spirit, the promised 'handler' of 'the things of Christ', promised as part of the ascension closure of 'time's sacrament' in its immediate incidence as then ready to be dependably available to all generations of its intended future.

Examples are many of how its interpretation suffers from the tensions or the failures among its heirs, or, indeed, from their perversity. In his *Grey Eminence*, Aldous Huxley drew the portrait of a Capuchin friar, a contemplative Christian who, out of his Frenchness and an avenue to influence, allowed himself to be seduced by the idea that the glory of God could be well advanced by the political interests of France as 'God's own country'. As 'the right hand man' of his Cardinal Richelieu, the friar bore responsibility for the horrors of a Thirty Years' War. The legend *Ad majorem gloriam Dei* can be a darkly seductive formula.

Or vigilance is needed where perceptions are more warped than vicious. The meaning of redemption, for example, can be so easily trivialised or distorted and people then have to be gently undeceived. Thus, a character in Murdoch's *A Word Child* sees the death of Jesus as 'a fairy tale of constructive suffering', 'that was magic alright' – a sort of fantasy, because 'God' could not die, and anyway, 'suffering blotting out sin' is pretending that 'somehow all is well'. No sense there of 'things vicarious', of sin as the world knows it, or of the call to live redemptively amidst its ravages.

Or 'ill report' – as Paul would call it – of this lofty order concerning an alleged 'out-of-date-ness' in faith or about 'people seeking refuge in churches looking for something that used to be found', when novels theologise awry, has to be patiently disproved. 'As deceivers and yet true' was how Paul caught this paradox of being read as false in the very art of being true. Loving God with all the mind has to care lest any 'deceived' are so by failure in its own loyalty. For faith is not had only for inward possession but as intending all in its length and breadth – those dimensions of its depth and height. It always needs the prayer of the psalmist: 'Let not those who seek Thee be confounded through me' (69:6). To be sure, he was referring then to a tragic situation he feared might have them argue that Yahweh had abandoned him. The theologian's anxiety has to be lest he should be as one through whom God was not truly measured.

It is exactly a right anxiety in the intellectual love of God which points our study to its other two dimensions. The 'love's exchange' between the Lord and the soul moves through mental tasks to be expressive and expending in the world of society. It is expressive in taking to the arts, being intimately sacramental in transacting the perceived sacrament God in Christ has set at the heart of divine love to humankind. Julian of Norwich had it the other way round:

> In the self-same point that our soul is made sensual in the self-same point
> is the City of God ordained to us from the beginning. I saw full surely that
> our substance is in God and also I saw that in our sensuality God is.

So the Passion takes up Bach's Chorales, the Creeds build Chartres, the Nativity is told by Rembrandt, a Christian art, through all its cultural forms, embraces all the Christian story. Expressive faith has been a nativity within Nativity, a passion to understand the Passion of the Lord in what might worthily explore it. Is it not recorded that Handel found himself in tears in the composing of The Hallelujah Chorus when, as he wrote, 'I saw all heaven opened'?

That, for many who are reserved or agnostic about the faith in Christ, beauty has come to have almost a religious quality is a strange paradox. George Eliot, following Emil Feuerbach whom she had translated from the German, felt that Christianity somehow 'tainted' love by having it supremely in a 'special history', whereas love should abjure all distinction between the human and divine, seeing it was itself divine human-ness, the 'God' of the only divineness there could be. We should be satisfied with love in its human bonds and, if we do not see 'the idea of God' there and only there, then abolish it altogether.

Such a view, like a 'rich young ruler' turning away, could be 'not far' from Christian, yet not where Christians come. Inter-human love is *per se* religious in its mystery and promise but only explicitly so if we know it as a clue to love of transcendent order, where the treacheries of our own are judged and its benedictions fully and duly enabled.

However, taking love via the clue of beauty as appealing to philosophers, brings them like that 'rich, young ruler' to the very heart of Christian faith, even if not asking 'What lack I yet?' Certainly there is a moral pull in good art: it can seem 'holy' in the fact of its esteem. Iris

Murdoch thought that attention to good art was a kind of praying, as a place where our self-centredness is transcended in the tribute of intelligent imagination. Robert Browning's "Tis we musicians know' is a very intelligent remark about the nature of worship, as also of musical appreciation. It is in line with John Donne's word about lovers as 'interassured of the mind' seeing that they had no need to distrust each other, asking in 'The Good Morrow' 'Who is so safe as we?' Art and love, whether in painting or poetry, in stone or colour, drama or design, are where soul possesses faith, once faith enters the soul.

To be sure, the unison may be fallible, since either may fail the other, as with wanderers round galleries or auditors at oratorios, who are only casually there. Even so, struggling faith may be in quest, if 'the readiness is all'. An expressive love, less than intellectual, will always fall short of what expression should attain. By its inherently sacramental character, Christianity has always known that nature has to be taken into association with it, seeing how far its faith in Incarnation belongs with its reading of the natural order as the creaturely realm of 'our low estate.' Is it then unworthy that the dating of 'the first Noel' should have coincided with a deep winter festival in the northern hemisphere? Or that the expressive Christ-love of Francis of Assisi, with his hymn of 'All creatures of our God and King', should have approved in 1223 the first Christmas crèche tradition?

Superstition, no doubt, could then emerge for mothers to think fertility might be theirs on 'Holy Night' – a different love of God from Anselm's logical necessity of the Incarnation.

The early Church did not celebrate the Feast of the Nativity, perhaps lest pagans should align it with a *natalis invicti* of imperial Rome. Origen held it a habit only of unregenerates. Certainly from the early Middle Ages it could even take over some obscenity. Bawdy ballads had a part in the origin of carols, with their rhetorical refrains and the release they gave to rural or to market revelry. *Natus est parvulus ergo venite* could have other meanings for the other-minded. The Church struggled with – and within – itself to curb or educate these unseemly celebrants of her mysteries, but had, in large measure to fall back on the wisdom Bede records in *The Ecclesiastical History of the English People*, as given by Pope Gregory to Archbishop Augustine of Canterbury. It was that, if the old heathen temples in Kent were well built, they should be retrieved for Christian worship by the sprinkling of holy water and exorcism thereby. Then they might serve Christian worshippers coming along familiar paths.

The 17th century puritans did not accept this logic when, by an interdiction, the Parliament of 1649 turned the feast into the fast of Christmas. Things of nature persist in penetrating into things of faith and 'the Word made flesh' that hallows them is popularly at stake with them. As for Christmas cards as really sacramental, they did not exist until mid 19th century. Perhaps, around Christ's Nativity, where emotions were less than serious, carols could be no more than whimsical, as with the familiar and much-loved 'bird and farmyard' carol, fitting the Latin of a Prudentius poem of Christmas to the creature voices.

These 'imperfect offices of prayer and praise' bring us again to the more worthy expressiveness of 'love's exchange' between the Lord and the soul in works that, in themselves, told faith in hallowing materials. The eastern art of the ikon, which so troubled some consciences before and after the rise of Islam, sacredly fulfilled the conscience of others. Their painting was meant as an act of prayer. The 'raw' materials – wood, oil, dye, pigment – were taken into a deliberate 'consecration' extending likewise to the time and care of their completion. The exercise of skill was a purpose to divine glory. The veneration of the finished ikon, which iconoclasts deplored, was a vehicle through which to pass into the worship of the Lord, original source of all that might become 'the work of human hands'. These had their consecration where faith found its witness, and both through dwelling in the history.

Iconography took up in visual art the theology of 'the face' as noted earlier in Paul's letter to Corinthians. The ikon loved the open face, shunning complete profile when the eyes could not be read because they were directed into absent distance. Whole figures were proper to the iconostasis, celebrating saints and martyrs but the face told all, concerning the Incarnate Word, whether in the tide of ministry or the climax of 'the man of sorrows'. Likewise 'the Mother Mary', as *Theotokos* – theology has urgent duty to hold the word *from* a meaning it could never have, *to* the sense in which we should know to use it. The ikon let its artistry contain that problem while the grace of Mary, the mystery of divine infancy, were legible in the contours of her face, her arms and bosom. There is no mistaking through the long centuries of Christian Europe, the themes of faith giving such rich motive skill to its artists and their patrons. As with all human stories, there were 'imperfections in these holy things'. Inanimate in their materiality, they were not the offering of 'unblemished lambs' but there was a love in them presenting for love's sake.

One feature of this 'love's exchange' in art is how culturally domestic it is in all its incidence across the centuries whether Coptic, Ethiopian, Greek, Italian, Dutch or Byzantine through all their moods and modes. The common theme of a Galilean nativity and a Passion in Roman Jerusalem takes portrayal in the idiom of any place and every time that think into its meaning. The theme, for its part, attains the interpretation it has itself imparted to the point where it is almost overwhelmed by the 'decoration' it receives – as notably in the baroque and the Italianate – and yet compellingly retains itself in being so far handled by diversity. If Leonardo Da Vinci could borrow the features of his local citizens to be disciples round the table, his 'The Last Supper' might be thought at risk in the fiction, while also true by the pledge (Revelation 3:20) to all would-be disciples 'I will sup with him and he with me'. For it was only once 'the last supper'.

With music and art, architecture, housing them both, has been an eloquent realm of 'love expressed', between 'the Christian Jesus' and the soul of faith. Even de-constructionists have drawn analogy from the architects in purporting to detect the 'structure' of words in which rational man contrives to presume a house of meaning which only language has built to delude him. More happily, a gentle wisdom can draw from 'essays in stone', basilicas and cathedrals or the lowly village church, the text of a love exchange in the sacramental form of edifice and fabric and beauty, cohering in a shape a faith ordained and brought to pass. Then the prophet's word: 'The zeal of Thy house' could have a monumental meaning in the rising arch and the buttressed-windowed walls.

There is that evident cruciformed pattern, those northern–southward transepts across the west and east of nave and choir and sanctuary, the village church that even seems to lean along its axis, resembling how and where 'Jesus laid his head'. The reasons may be purely practical but the imagery poetically belongs. These haunts of Christian worship bear the stamp of one their worship loves. They tell in structured sacrament of skill, design and ordered space the structure of 'time's sacrament', and, so doing, recruit time still by durability to give it word, so that even 'so many dead may lie around', gathered to its meaning in their generations.

Where time is captured in its length, space is hallowed where it is created in protecting walls and under soaring arches. Music can there be sung in different keys.

> Joy in its crafting, all around I see,
> Truth so enduring, dwell I with Thee.

The arch has always been seen as prime image both of faith and love, as also of marriage. Whether rounded or pointed, Eastern or Gothic, there are two arms, the one a meaning offered, the other a meaning received and each inter-changing those destined roles, so that both alike are reaching *to* and reaching *for* the partnering. Then the keystone binds the two in one, space is shaped below where 'light and shade repose and music dwells'. If folk are bored in pews they can look to the sermon in the arch. All is a miracle of teasing gravity, so that vaulting ribs and fanning veins hold up what fills the intervening spaces so that all is duly ceiled.

[125]

All vaulting masonry is surface for 'craftsmen's art' and decoration serves alike for adornment and utility. There is a consecration of engineering or, rather, engineering becomes consecration, so that there is a perpetual sacrament of the proper destiny of all material as belonging both to an economic and a spiritual order. We are believing the more in 'the community of holy things', as accompanying the *communio sanctorum* of the pedestrian order. We can re-write the hymn about 'the sinking sun', the threnody on 'naked shingles of the world', and rejoice in the solidity of incarnation.

For the will to build – in these terms – had its origin in the cradle of God in Christ. Doubtless, churches and cathedrals have other uses, as symbols – like Durham – of some guardian of power by frontiers of pride, or to prove – like Liverpool – that not only Normans knew the art. Human motives, always mixed, are never pure yet the purity they reach for tells its name through all compromise of sin. Where 'prayer is wont to be made' sets the sign of its steeple on the rural landscape commenting on the point of things. There is patience, too, in those vicarious buttresses, taking the burden so that less solid walls leave ample place for light and tracery. So they lean at right-angles to enable what otherwise they do not share.

All within, modest and small, or massive and awesome, conveys by its form towards an ultimate sanctuary, not cynically, 'the holy end' to leave the rest as vulgar but integral with meaning, where what is sacramental around is 'consecrate' in 'bread and wine', where there is access into celebration of the source of all. There is through all a discernible 'love exchange' in the several shapes of inward soul and outward hand and sight.

Meanwhile, the windows – the art of telling it in colour via glass when light itself is enlisted, a calligraphy to make imagination literate with scenes 'according to the Scriptures', or – these apart – to let colour speak as colour may. Where light is not merely on, but through, it becomes the surest pattern of the Incarnation, of 'the life that is the light of men'. The tracery that frames it becomes in turn a faint analogy of credal words.

'Zeal of Thy house', then, all in all, is clue to tell the will and skill to build, the large expenditure of pains and patience in the worth of wood and sound and form and craft that came by it, as a 'zeal' of love before it was a 'zeal' of mind and hand. A house of Christian worship is a statement of intent. It is not well regarded as an auditorium, yet it is due place for another sort of sacrament within 'the message of the walls'. That other is the vocal sort, the disciplined zeal of 'truth through personality' that belongs with 'the ministry of the Word'. Rhetoric these days is a thing to suspect or despise like the word 'theology' used to denote tedious obscurity wilfully pursued. Sermons are rarely themes of enthusiasm. Yet there are few sacraments serving the central sacrament of time more apt than ordered discourse telling truth from the heart with the warmth of unambiguous fervour.

This brings us round to earlier accent on 'intellectual love' but not now of the private, secret, cerebral kind but one which, out of these, commends its themes with an exegesis that is at once a *confessio*. Then the content of the faith translates into the burden of a ready mind and is heard in accents of conviction. Such preaching – a word for which the New Testament shows much enthusiasm – is the due 'zeal of the faith' known in human telling.

It has to be a telling which engages with hearers where they are and mediates the meaning that is felt within. In the Anglican tradition – and its architecture – there is always a distinction between a 'lectern' where Scriptures are read and a 'pulpit' where they are interpreted. Thus there is no 'according to a Scripture' that is not 'according to some Scriptured one', versed in some measure in the wealth of its vocabulary and the treasury of its verbal life. Such scholarship in ministry is not to the exclusion of individual concern and study but its encouragement out of the holy erudition of – it is hoped – 'a learned ministry'.

All then becomes part of 'love's exchange', spiritual traffic between minds and a spirited exercise of love to Christ in a dedicated open converse with his mind. 'The tongue of one learned . . . to know how to speak . . .' and speak 'to the weary' was a great prophet's plea (Isaiah 50:4). As 'iron sharpens iron' so fervour kindles where there are live coals. These for Isaiah elsewhere belonged with human lips, where faith is told from a passion in the heart.

Yet, lacking that sincerity, words may be a tactic of evasion. The 'love exchange' between the Lord and the soul, intellectual and expressive in the ways we have reviewed must become also 'endeavour and expense', as memorably told by W. H. Vanstone, in a book with that title a quarter century ago. There are agnostics who fear that faith is only a sanctioned egoism, as if Paul, for example, had said: 'To live is me', whereas it was 'To me to live is Christ' (Philippians 1:21).

'To discover a religion in which it was possible to love' was one day Nietzsche's aspiration, in seeming aberration from the philosophy usually associated with his name. Could he have phrased a surer definition of Christian faith as the faith of divine Incarnation, of an Incarnation with a ministry at its heart and told as 'the compassion of a 'most moved Mover', creator of the heavens and earth? That 'sojourn' of the Eternal, a tent-pitcher among us, had disclosed the world as a crucifying place. It showed that service in it would have that shape too. The teacher called disciples to an active school in which they were more than spectators of his ministry. Strangely he associated what supervened for him at its close with his invitation to them at the start.

Of Jesus, Oscar Wilde remarked that 'he creates the mood in which alone he can be understood' – a sentiment in line with the entire argument of these Chapters that Jesus 'authored' in his disciples the faith they 'authored' concerning him. The 'authority' in both ways was more, much more, than 'mood'. For 'mood' is a fickle word: 'mind' would better fit but 'will' best of all. Within the intellectual love we have pondered and through the expressive love that makes a poetry of the faith, 'will' is the ultimate dimension.

Much ethicism, ancient and modern, has thought of 'human society' as the sufficient ground and source of goodness. Then the idea of God is no more than a surrogate for a goodness that is entirely human. What can 'love is of God' mean seeing that love's sphere, love's origin, are wholly with and for the human scene? Why the theological dimension, imported to commend or to sustain it?

Perhaps the answer to such deserving questions lies in the very nature of the sacramental which belongs precisely to the human-ness which the questions plead. Patently, we are not self-sufficient in the created world of nature, for all the empire it imparts. What have we that we did not receive? we are bound to ask at every point, surveying history, assessing nature, or transacting in society. These intimations of indebtedness, as in a world of obligation, position us in a relatedness that inter-human society neither originated nor exhausts. To sense this more than 'social' quality of our awareness as selves-in-being or – better – this ever 'social' quality in its wider context, is to enter on the sacramental nature of all things in our ken. Our liability is to being itself, not merely to the economic, the familial, the social and the civic. We mean, in our selfhoods, more than barter in the market, orbit in society, cogs in a machine or characters in a novel. That 'more' is our liability to belong inclusively which, in turn, is to behave sacramentally. To know it so is to be given back to the acknowledgement of God, and of that situation so read as 'a purpose of love'.

Would it then be strange to surmise that what this reading took as the character of our situation would not lack a purpose of love to serve its fulfilment when history proved how far short we fell of it? That would argue the sort of sacramental history we have studied in Christ, coming where we are but from within the responsible eternity from which – as we argued – all things derived that they might be the sacramental they are, and as faith receives them.

Such love, once recognised, would be the supreme incentive to its emulation, because we had realised it as the sure interpretation of ourselves. We would then be beyond a humanism that thought to confine love only to things between ourselves. We have it enlarged into a mandate more compelling and a warrant more inclusive. The sacrament of 'God with us', this 'Emmanuel', makes sacrament of personality in all the reaches of experience, making us participant in the work of love in the world.

Then to know is to will and to will is to do. 'The cup of cold water', in the Name of the Lord, 'the oil and the wine in the wound', and 'the pence at the inn' – all these are the sacraments from 'the Word made flesh'. They are how 'he dwells in us and we in him'.

They were, and their emulation will remain, directly personal, local and immediate. For us now they have also to translate into the business of the citizen to care about the exploitative nature of high finance moved only by the profit motive; the desperate imbalance in the patterns of the world, as between poverty and consumerism, deprivation and privilege, chronic disadvantage and blatant elegance.

How is 'love's exchange' of worship, art, poetry, song and liturgy between the Lord and the soul, to be 'without hypocrisy' in a world where one child in five, in the poorest countries, dies before that age through water-borne disease and lack of sanitation; where economic forces are set to aggravate the ills of ignorance, illiteracy, migration and poverty; where the most reputedly 'Christian' nation baulks global measures of redress and salvation, by cruel prioritising of its own vested interests congenially interpreting the world?

Christian mission has been, for generations, a central expression of the love between the Church and Christ. It has long indeed exemplified how love can only serve, and how only love can serve, in due 'obedience of faith'. Such, on God's part and ours, is the supreme commendation the Gospel gives and takes. As word and witness it abides, but there is clear contemporary call to have all quest for human answer in 'I believe . . . my personal Saviour . . .' move also into a care for how other religions take up the global human crisis that 'World Summits' sanguinely debate. For every faith is deeply implicated in the cultures and societies to which the issues belong. No single religion has the range of reach into the urgency in practical terms, none has monopoly of action even if they assume uniqueness in the answer. How each and all of them handle environment, connive with selfishness, corrupt good faith, expound gentleness and interpret human hope and tragedy – are questions that must seek a common answer and find a common front. That drive they must concert also with every ardent scepticism and where-ever also secularity cares.

Thus our 'love exchange' with 'the Christian Jesus' takes us into liability to all religions and – as far as may – with them. 'Take my yoke' had to do with all that was 'wearied and heavy laden' – a condition apt to so many in this victim-having, victim-making world. It follows that a large dimension of any Christian mission now is its community, of thought and action, in ministry to 'the miseries of the world' and how that world 'might be saved' insofar as economics, politics, law and ethics through all societies belong with that 'salvation'.

Chief Rabbi Jonathan Sachs has recently written about 'the dignity of difference'. It is a splendid formula in that 'difference' should always be mutually 'dignified'. But what of 'difference' that disputes, or even disallows, the human 'dignity'? Tolerance cannot well be another word for indifference. Robert Browning has the point in his 'Christmas Eve':

> This tolerance is a genial mood! . . .
> A value for religion's self
> A carelessness about the sects of it,
> Let me enjoy my own convictions,
> Nor watch my neighbour's faith with fretfulness . . .

'Convictions' for 'enjoyment' are thereby suspect and need the honesty placed also in their commendation. So it was on Browning's Christmas Eve, alike in life and logic. He wanted 'Christ confessed as the God of salvation', the 'salvation' in God's own definition.

From that faith there is endless differing religiously and otherwise, as there was of old for Jesus when 'There was division because of him' (John 7:43, 9:16 and 10:19). The spiritual elements as to faith that all diversity presents are best taken into the action of ministry inside all human wrong, into a politics of compassion against all tyranny and injustice. Only there will each have the credentials of the others to be on behalf of God or of the God on whose behalf they are. For, in measure, we become like what we worship. The 'Whom' where all faiths come in worship they have in that worship's keeping.

Then 'Our Lord Jesus Christ' – though intensely known as ours – is no privatising formula. It is the confession of an inclusive Lord, in knowledge of the love of God, pledged by its own nature to its own fidelity, and unreservedly entrusted to ours.

Index of Themes

Index of Names and Terms

Biblical References